A COMPLETE
SOURCE BOOK FOR THE
LORD'S SUPPER

D1365012

A COMPLETE SOURCE BOOK FOR THE LORD'S SUPPER

CHARLES L. WALLIS, EDITOR

BAKER BOOK HOUSE
Grand Rapids, Michigan

Third printing, May 1981

Special acknowledgment is made to the following who have granted permission for the reprinting of copyrighted material from the books listed below:

ABINGDON PRESS for "The Quest" from *Be Still and Know* by Georgia Harkness, copyright 1953 by Pierce & Washabaugh; extract from *The Beginnings of Christianity* by Clarence Tucker Craig, copyright 1943 by Whitmore & Stone; extract from *The Christ of Every Road* by E. Stanley Jones, copyright 1930 by E. Stanley Jones; extracts from *Communion Meditations*, edited by Gaston Foote, copyright 1951 by Pierce & Smith; extract from *Fight the Good Fight* by Robert Menzies, copyright 1949 by Pierce & Smith; extract from *The Fine Art of Public Worship* by Andrew W. Blackwood, copyright 1939 by Whitmore & Smith; extract from *The Life and Teachings of Jesus* by Charles M. Laymon, copyright 1955 by Pierce & Washabaugh; extracts from *Lift Up Your Hearts,* enl. ed., by Walter Russell Bowie, copyright 1939, 1956 by Pierce & Washabaugh; "When Jesus Washed the Feet of Judas" from *More Hilltop Verses and Prayers* by Ralph S. Cushman, copyright 1949 by Pierce & Smith; extracts from *Prayer* by George A. Buttrick, copyright 1942 by Whitmore & Stone; extract from *Rediscovering the Words of Faith* by Charles T. Sardeson, copyright 1956 by Pierce & Washabaugh; extract from *The Transforming Friendship* by Leslie D. Weatherhead, published by Abingdon Press; extract from *Ultimate Questions* by Nathaniel Micklem, copyright 1955 by Pierce & Washabaugh; extracts from *The Word in Season* by Hughes Wagner, copyright 1951 by Pierce & Smith.

ASSOCIATION PRESS for extract from *Book of Student Prayers* by Jack Finegan; extract from *Rediscovering the Church* by George Laird Hunt; extract from *That One Face* by Richard Roberts.

BASIL BLACKWELL for extract from *The Eucharistic Words of Jesus* by Joachim Jeremias, reprinted by permission of Basil Blackwell and The Macmillan Company.

BEACON PRESS for extract from *Services of Religion.*

THE BETHANY PRESS for "An Order of Worship for a Candlelight Com-

Christian Doctrine of the Lord's Supper by Robert M. Adamson; extracts from *Religious Values in the Sacraments* by H. J. Wotherspoon; extract from *The Sacraments of the New Testament* by John C. Lambert.

THE UNITED LUTHERAN CHURCH IN AMERICA for "Lord Jesus Christ, We Humbly Pray" by Henry E. Jacobs from *Common Service Book,* copyright 1917, 1918 by the United Lutheran Church in America.

THE UPPER ROOM for "Meditation for Holy Communion" by Russell Q. Chilcote and "Upper Room Communion Hymm" by Frederick M. Morley from *The Upper Room Pulpit,* copyright and reprinted by permission of The Upper Room and the authors.

THE WESTMINSTER PRESS for extracts from *The Altar Fire* by Olive Wyon, 1954; communion service from *The Book of Common Worship,* copyright 1946 by the Board of Christian Education of the Presbyterian Church, in the USA; extract from *Christian Love in Everyday Living* by Owen Hutchison, copyright 1955 by W. L. Jenkins; extract from *Early Christian Fathers (Library of Christian Classics, I);* extract from *The Great Invitation* by Emil Brunner, tr. by Harold Knight, 1955; extract from *Guests of God* by John F. Jansen, copyright 1956 by W. L. Jenkins; extracts from *Institutes of the Christian Religion* by John Calvin, tr. by John Allen; extract from *Jesus* by Martin Dibelius, tr. by Charles B. Hedrick and Frederick C. Grant, copyright 1949 by W. L. Jenkins; extract from *Making Sense Out of Life* by Charles Duell Kean, copyright 1954 by W. L. Jenkins; extract from *The Significance of the Church* by Robert M. Brown, copyright 1956 by W. L. Jenkins; extract from *Tradition, Freedom and the Spirit* by Daniel Jenkins, 1951; extract from *The Unity of the Bible* by H. H. Rowley, 1956.

Special acknowledgment is also made to the following persons for permission to reprint the materials indicated:

George A. Buttrick for General Service II, used at the Madison Avenue Presbyterian Church, New York City, and based on traditional sources.

Leslie Savage Clark for her poems, "Bread" and "Remembrance."

Walter Lowrie for extract from *The Short Story of Jesus* by Walter Lowrie, published in 1943 by Charles Scribner's Sons and copyright by Walter Lowrie.

Harold F. Humbert for extract from his poem, "Sanctuary."

Ida Norton Munson for her poems, "Oldest Deacon" and "The Road to Emmaus," from *The Surgeon's Hands,* copyright 1944 by Bruce Humphries, Inc.

Kirby Page for "Whoso Suffers Most" by Harriet Eleanor King from *Living Prayerfully,* edited and copyright 1941 by Kirby Page and published by Rinehart & Co., Inc.

Eleanor Slater for her poem, "Communion," from *Why Hold the Hound?,* copyright and published in 1941 by Henry Harrison.

John W. Suter for litany from *Devotional Offices for General Use,* edited by John W. Suter and published in 1928 by The Century Company.

To my twin brother
ORTHELLO L. WALLIS

PREFACE

On the night in which he was betrayed, Jesus broke bread with his disciples. They had often shared a common board, but that night he ascribed to the ordinary loaf and chalice a significance to which devotion has ever clung.

Jesus anticipated thoughtfully that last hour of fellowship, hoping that the simple rite might become a vessel by which he should be remembered. Through the intervening years the church has gloriously adorned his words and actions of that night with the beauty and majesty of ritual and poetry. In each repetition of the Supper the faith of his followers is renewed, we commune with him and through him with Christian brethren of whatever generation and shore.

The whole gospel is dramatized in this ordinance of bread and wine. The Supper has been variously identified as the eucharist, the sacrament, holy communion, the memorial, the sacrifice, the offering, or, more simply, as the breaking of bread. These designations suggest the breadth of understandings attributed to the Supper and each in its way emphasizes particular aspects of an ordinance that speaks to human needs and yearnings as does no other act of faith and worship. Here is shown forth Christ's giving and our receiving. Here are his people made one in recollection, in worship and in commitment. Here we witness anew his incarnation, his life and ministry, his death and resurrection. Here we sense a Presence which time has not dimmed, and we rise on wings of faith to discern that hour when all men of faith shall share in the heavenly feast provided for those who love him. Leslie D. Weatherhead thoughtfully counsels:

I suggest that we should partake of it and let it come to mean to us whatever God can make it mean to people constituted as we are. To some . . . it is merely an act of remembrance. To others it is a sacramentum, an oath of allegiance. To another it symbolizes his death. Another argues that as bread and wine nourish our physical body, so it is the very being of Christ himself, received into the soul, that nourishes it and makes it live and grow, and that the elements symbolize this fact. They think of him as the Bread of Life. Most of us find that material things can be channels by which a reality is reached greater than the means which produce it, or our understanding of the process, even as lovely music induces a state of soul, an end far greater than the means which produce it. Surely, we must come to the service and allow it to mean for us whatever our faith can make it mean.

This Supper, since the early days of the church, has been central in worship and piety. From every era of church history have come testimonies relevant to the meaning and value of the ordinance. More than three hundred years ago Robert Bruce wrote:

I say we get no other thing in the sacrament than we get in the Word. Content thee with this. But suppose it be so, yet the sacrament is not superfluous. But wouldst thou understand what new thing thou gettest—what other thing thou gettest. I will tell thee. . . . I say, we get Christ better than we did before; we get the thing that we got more fully, that is, with a surer apprehension than we had of it before; we get a better grip of Christ now. For by the sacrament my faith is nourished, the bounds of my soul are enlarged; and so, when I had but a little grip of Christ before, as it were betwixt my finger and my thumb, now I get him in my whole hand; and aye the more that my faith grows, the better grip I get of Jesus Christ.

In *The Maner of the Lord's Supper,* John Knox wrote:

For the ende of our comming thyther is not to make protestation that we are upright and juste in our lives, but contrariwise. Let us consider, then, that this sacrament is a singular medicine for all poore sicke creatures, a comfortable helpe to weak soules, and that our Lord requireth no other worthiness on our parte, but that we unfaynedly acknowledge our noghtines and imperfection.

The Supper is a tie that binds all hearts to Christ and to one another. Yet this service, so simple in its origins, has been the source of baffling contention and bewildering division. The one service in which all Christains participate is an instrument that has separated men. To be sure, the varying interpretations evidence the significance that the service has held for all generations. Such diversity in Christian experience makes it improbable that Christians shall ever define the Supper with precise agreement, nor is it essential that they do. What is basic to our appreciation of the ordinance is that all men find their Lord at his hallowed table and that they read well the mind of him who welcomed all manner of men to that circle of love where first he shared his broken body. Those men, save Judas only, found in him a center of devotion and loyalty and so rose above their divergent temperaments, traditions and testimonies. That centrality of emphasis is the need of the Christian community of our day, and we too shall find it as we sit at the common table.

At this table Christ's guests of whatever creed or heritage find their spirits kindled, their devotion renewed and deepened, their commitment made stalwart and brave, and their lives linked in a fellowship of love and camaraderie. What matter then that the individuals at the table find in their hearts a vocabulary others may not speak?

II

Lloyd C. Douglas in *The Big Fisherman* creates a vivid picture of the Last Supper which he describes as "a most depressing feast" in which "the fear that had haunted the disciples for many days was now confirmed. . . . The disciples were heartsick. . . . They were all weeping." Certainly at that time there were sober reflection and solemn apprehension. The disciples were not sure what the morrow would bring. But the heart of Jesus, if we may judge from his discourses as recorded especially in John's gospel, was full of love and hope. And later, when the disciples met again in the glow of the Easter triumph and then again and again in moments of trial and stress and storm, the service became the eucharist, a rite of joyous thanksgiving and praise.

This note at times seems lost in our churches. The Supper seems dull and perfunctory, without lustre or real meaning. Often this service seems oppressively routine and grave, and it is invariably identified with that in the Christian experience which is melancholy. When such attitudes prevail, the genuineness of the Supper for Christ and his disciples has been lost.

A congregation's enthusiasm for attending the Supper is likely to mirror the enthusiasm of him who officiates. And the pastor's appreciation of this service needs the continual nurture of prayerful reflection and thoughtful study. John Henry Jowett in his Yale lectures of two generations ago cautioned his colleagues of the peril of *deadening familiarity with the sublime:*

You will not have been long in the ministry before you discover that it is possible to be fussily busy about the Holy Place and yet to lose the wondering sense of the Holy Lord. We may have much to do with religion and yet not be religious. We may become mere guide-posts when we were intended to be guides. We may indicate the way, and yet not be found in it. We may be professors but not pilgrims. Our studies may be workshops instead of "upper rooms." Our share in the table-provisions may be that of analysts rather than guests. We may become so absorbed in words that we forget the Word.

St. Paul wisely urges self-examination prior to communion. In an earlier day abundant opportunities for self-examination and preparation were incorporated into the framework of the church program. The mid-week meeting, prayer sessions, sacramental gatherings are now less frequently attended. Although compensations for these are impossible, a minister may use or introduce ways by which his people may approach the Supper with a readiness of mind and spirit.

Surely, if the Supper is observed infrequently—bi-monthly or quarterly —a sermon on the previous Sunday may be devoted to an interpretation of the Supper. A pastor on occasion may have the table prepared for a church school or youth group and he may show, step by step, the rite's significance according to biblical fundamentals and the witness of the church. Small children at the time of their baptism or confirmation usually receive sufficient instruction concerning the Supper—and that instruction somehow is expected to last for a lifetime!

Observance of the Supper may be identified with the corresponding season in the church calendar. The worship, scriptural readings, hymns and anthems, and prayers, may highlight the Supper's relation to such times as Advent, the New Year, Lent, Brotherhood Week, and World Communion Sunday. Special times when communion may be appropriately held include Christmas Eve services, New Year Watch Night, Ash Wednesday, Maundy Thursday, and for Sunday breakfasts for church men, women or children, at summer camps and assemblies and various inter-church conferences and conventions. For many of these activities nothing seems more suitable as a culmination to study and fellowship. Caution, however, should be taken lest the Supper be used merely to fill-in a program or to serve communion without an adequate and considered preparation.

Usually when the Supper is observed in a church, the pastor or duly designated persons take communion to the members who are sick or shut-in. This custom, long practiced by many branches of Christendom and warranted by the example of the early church, is becoming more and more common among the evangelical churches. The Supper is, of course, a fitting time for baptism and the reception of new members. Of ancient vintage is the practice of marking one or more communions during the year for the remembering of parishioners who have recently died.

The receiving of a special communion collection in behalf of the less fortunate members of the church or for other benevolent purposes follows the example of the early Christian fellowships. It is often desirable to combine this with the regular offering. Church members quickly become accustomed to the use of communion offering envelopes and will give as generously as though two separate offerings were taken.

III

This anthology brings together worship and homiletic resources representative of the wide-ranging history of Christianity. Although this volume includes much critical, theological and interpretative matter, the selections have been made on the basis of usefulness in worship and preaching. Four major divisions are followed by indexes of texts cited, poetry, special days and occasions, names of contributors and sources from which materials have been reprinted, and subjects. All scriptures not otherwise indicated are from the King James Version. An asterisk (*) indicates adaptation or abbreviation.

The editor is grateful to Mrs. Frances V. Wilkins, librarian of the Keuka College Library, who made many books available through inter-library loan from the libraries at the Princeton Theological Seminary, Union Theological Seminary and Cornell University. Considerable assistance was given by the personnel of the Colgate Rochester Divinity School Library, the Rochester Public Library and the University of Rochester Library.

CONTENTS

PREFACE   *xi*

I. COMMUNION SERVICES   *1*
  A. General Services   *3*
  B. Service Following Morning or Evening Worship   *9*
  C. A Scriptural Service   *11*
  D. A Candlelight Service   *14*
  E. A Service for a Summer Conference   *15*
  F. A Service for the Sick and Shut-in   *16*
  G. Communion Scriptures   *19*
  H. Calls to Worship and Opening Sentences   *20*
  I. Invocations and Opening Prayers   *23*
  J. Benedictions and Closing Prayers   *26*
  K. Communion Music   *28*
        1. Hymns   *28*
        2. Anthems   *30*
        3. Organ   *31*
        4. Communion Services   *32*

II. A SHEAF OF COMMUNION PRAYERS   *33*
  A. Pastoral Prayers   *35*
  B. Prayers before the Supper   *43*
  C. Prayers after the Supper   *49*
  D. Litanies and Responsive Prayers   *51*
  E. Church Covenants and Affirmations of Faith   *58*

**III. RESOURCES FOR COMMUNION PREACHING
AND COMMUNION TABLE MEDITATIONS   *65***
  A. Meanings of the Supper   *67*
  B. Light from the Upper Room   *79*

C. Christ, the Table's Host   *85*

D. Of Bread and Wine   *89*

E. On Symbols and Sacraments   *94*

F. In the Breaking of Bread   *100*

G. This Do in Remembrance   *104*

H. Rite of the Covenant   *108*

I. He Laid Down His Life   *111*

J. God's Action—*and Ours*   *116*

K. Fellowship of Faith   *120*

L. That They May Be One   *124*

M. Unto the Ends of the Earth   *131*

N. Marriage Supper of the Lamb   *139*

O. Sacrament of the Towel and Basin   *142*

P. The Hand of the Betrayer   *145*

Q. And They Sang a Hymn   *149*

R. Testimony of the Reformation   *153*

S. The Genius of Da Vinci   *159*

T. The Heart's Preparation   *162*

IV. *A TREASURY OF COMMUNION POETRY*   *167*

INDEX OF TEXTS   *199*

INDEX OF POETRY: POETS, TITLES AND FIRST LINES   *203*

INDEX OF DAYS AND SEASONS   *209*

INDEX OF AUTHORS AND SOURCES   *213*

INDEX OF SUBJECTS   *221*

I. Communion Services

A. GENERAL SERVICES

1 *General Service—1*

Organ Prelude

Hymn, *which may be a processional. If desired, the hymn may follow* **the** *call to worship.*

Call to Worship

Invocation *or* Prayer of Confession

The Lord's Prayer, *in unison*

Anthem, Solo *or* Hymn

Scripture Lesson

Offertory

[Hymn]

Sermon *or* Communion Meditation

Invitation, *to be said by the minister, before coming to the table, in these or other suitable words*:

> We are now about to observe the ordinance of the Lord's Supper. This table of the Lord is open to all fellow Christians; and although none should partake of these sacred emblems impenitent or without faith in Christ, we cordially invite all who are sincerely seeking him to come to his table, in the assurance that he who came into **the** world to be the Savior of all will in no wise cast them out.

> Come to this sacred table, not because you must, but because you may; come to testify not that you are righteous, but that you sincerely love our Lord Jesus Christ, and desire to be his true disciples; come, not because you are strong, but because you are weak; not because you have any claim on heaven's rewards, but because in your frailty and sin you stand in constant need of heaven's mercy and help; come, not to express an opinion, but to seek a Presence and pray for a Spirit.

[Reading of Names of Candidates for Membership

> *The candidates will come forward and take seats in front of* **the** *pulpit during the singing of the following hymn.*]

3

Communion Hymn

During the hymn, the cloth covering the elements should be carefully removed by the deacons.

[Reception of New Members]

[Reading of the Church Covenant *or* Affirmation of Faith]

[Gloria Patri]

Words of Institution, *to be said by the minister, standing before the table*:

The Lord Jesus in the night in which he was betrayed took bread (*here the minister may take the plate in his hands*); and when he had given thanks, he brake it, and said, This is my body, which is for you: this do in remembrance of me. In like manner also the cup (*here the minister may take the cup in his hands*), after supper, saying, This cup is the new covenant in my blood: this do, as often as ye drink it, in remembrance of me. For as often as ye eat this bread, and drink the cup, ye proclaim the Lord's death till he come.

The Giving of the Bread, *by the minister to the deacons or other assistants to distribute to the people, the minister saying as he does so*:

Jesus said, This is my body which is broken for you.

It is customary for the minister to be served first. After the people have been served, the minister will serve the deacons. But let none eat of the bread until the minister shall indicate by pronouncing one of the following two paragraphs:

Let us eat of this bread in remembrance of Christ; and may the life which was in him be in us also.

The body of our Lord Jesus Christ, which was given for thee, preserve thee unto everlasting life. Take and eat this in remembrance that Christ died for thee, and feed on him in thy heart by faith with thanksgiving.

Silent Prayer

The Giving of the Cup

Let the wine be distributed after the same manner as the bread, the minister repeating as he gives the cups to the deacons:

Jesus said, This cup is the new covenant in my blood.

When all have been served, let the minister, before partaking of the cup, pronounce one of the following two paragraphs:

Let us drink of this cup in remembrance of Christ; and may the spirit in which he died be our spirit.

The blood of our Lord Jesus Christ, which was shed for thee, preserve thee unto everlasting life. Drink this in remembrance that Christ's blood was shed for thee, and be thankful.

Silent Prayer

[Reading of the Names of Members of the Church Who Have Died Since the Last Communion

I heard a voice from heaven saying, Write, Blessed are the dead who die in the Lord from henceforth: yea, saith the Spirit, that they may rest from their labors; for their works follow with them.]

[Prayer of Gratitude for the Lives of the Deceased and of Consolation for the Bereaved]

[Offering for the Needy

The announcement of the offering may be made by repeating one or more of the following sentences:

As we have therefore opportunity, let us do good unto all men, especially unto them who are of the household of faith.

Whoso hath this world's good, and seeth his brother have need, and shutteth up his compassion from him, how dwelleth the love of God in him?

Ye know the grace of our Lord Jesus Christ, that, though he was rich, yet for your sakes he became poor, that ye through his poverty might become rich.]

Hymn

And when they had sung a hymn, they went out.

Benediction

Now the God of peace, that brought again from the dead our Lord Jesus, that great Shepherd of the sheep, through the blood of the everlasting covenant, make you perfect in every good work to do his will, working in you that which is well-pleasing in his sight, through Jesus Christ; to whom be glory forever and ever. Amen.

Organ Postlude

James Dalton Morrison

2 *General Service—2*

Organ Prelude
Call to Worship

The hour cometh and now is, when the true worshiper shall worship the Father in spirit and in truth: for the Father seeketh such to worship him.

Hymn of Praise

Invocation and the Lord's Prayer

Scripture Lesson

Reception of Members

Pastoral Prayer

Hymn

Sermon

Hymn

The Holy Communion

Minister: If any man sin, we have an advocate with the Father, Jesus Christ the righteous: and he is the propitiation for our sins; and not for ours only, but for the sins of the whole world. Wherefore ye that do truly and earnestly repent of your sins, and are in love and charity with your neighbors, and intend to lead a new life, following the commandments of God, and walking henceforth in his holy ways, draw near with faith, and take this holy sacrament to your comfort; and make your confession to almighty God.

Minister and people: Almighty and most merciful Father: we have erred, and strayed from thy ways like lost sheep. We have followed too much the devices and desires of our own hearts. We have offended against thy holy laws. We have left undone those things which we ought to have done: and we have done those things which we ought not to have done. But thou, O Lord, have mercy upon us. Spare thou those, O God, who confess their faults. Restore thou those who are penitent, according to thy promise declared unto mankind in Christ Jesus, our Lord. And grant, O most merciful Father, for his sake, that we may hereafter live a godly, righteous and sober life, to the glory of thy holy name. Amen.

Minister: Hear what comfortable words our Savior Christ saith unto all that truly turn to him: "Come unto me all ye that labor and are heavy laden, and I will give you rest. Blessed are they that do hunger and thirst after righteousness for they shall be filled." Therefore, lift up your hearts in peace and joy.

People: We lift them up unto the Lord.

Minister: Let us give thanks unto the Lord God.

People: It is meet and right so to do.

Minister: It is very meet, right and our bounden duty that we should at all times and in all places give thanks unto thee, O Lord, Holy Father, Almighty, Everlasting God. Therefore with angels and archangels and with all the company of heaven, we laud and magnify thy glorious name; evermore praising thee, and saying: Holy, holy, holy, Lord God of hosts, heaven and earth are full of thy glory. Glory be to thee, O Lord, most high.

Choir Hymn

Consecration of the Bread and Distribution by the Deacons

The body of our Lord Jesus Christ, which was given for thee, preserve thy soul and body unto everlasting life. Take and eat this in remembrance that Christ died for thee, and feed on him in thy heart by faith, with thanksgiving.

Consecration of the Cup and Distribution by the Deacons

The blood of our Lord Jesus Christ, which was shed for thee, preserve thy soul and body unto everlasting life. Take and eat this in remembrance that Christ's blood was shed for thee, and be thankful.

Communion Offering (*for those who are in need*)

Offertory Chant

Dedication of the Offering

Hymn

Benediction and Nunc Dimittis

Organ Postlude

3 *General Service—3*

Organ Prelude and Meditation

Hymn: "Light of the World, we hail thee."

Call to Worship

Minister: We are children of the sunrise and the morning gathered here as followers of him who with the fewest hours accomplished thy divinest work.

People: O Lord, send out thy light and thy truth, let them lead us to thy holy hill.

Minister: We have come into this our upper room in devout and loving memory of the Master who, one shadowed evening in the long ago, gave to his disciples the symbols of the holy grail and broken bread.

People: O thou who madest the out-goings of the morning and the evening to rejoice, keep us in thy holy love this day and forever more.

Minister: In company with all our fellow pilgrims of the spiritual life, and in the face of all the turmoil and difficulty of our days, we confess our faith in things unseen and yet eternal and our abiding hope in goodness, truth and beauty.

All: We believe in the fatherhood of God and in the brotherhood of man. We believe that Christ is the way and the truth and the life. We believe in the clean heart and the unworldly life, and in the service of love that Jesus exemplified. We accept his spirit and his teaching and dedicate ourselves to his unfinished work.　Amen.

Hymn: "Dear Lord and Father of Mankind."

Minister: Hear what comfortable words our Savior Christ saith unto all that truly turn to him: "Come unto me, all ye that labor and are heavy laden and I will give you rest." "If any man hear my voice and open the door, I will come in to him and will sup with him." Therefore lift up your hearts with peace and joy.

People: We lift them up unto the Lord.

Minister: Let us give thanks unto the Lord.

People: It is meet and right so to do.

Minister: For thy presence within us, O God, and for this sacrament of thy dear Son that our souls may be made clear and that we may evermore dwell in him and he in us.　Amen.

The Words of Institution

The Blessing and Administration of the Bread and of the Cup

Hymn: "Rise up, O men of God."

Benediction

Organ Postlude

Albert W. Palmer

B. SERVICE FOLLOWING MORNING OR EVENING WORSHIP

4 Hymn: "Break thou the Bread of Life"

Invitation

> Jesus said unto them, I am the bread of life: he that cometh to me shall never hunger; and he that believeth on me shall never thirst. . . . Him that cometh to me I will in no wise cast out.

Sharing of the Loaf

> For I have received of the Lord that which also I delivered unto you, That the Lord Jesus the same night in which he was betrayed took bread: and when he had given thanks, he brake it, and said, Take, eat: this is my body, which is broken for you: this do in remembrance of me.

> With this bread broken, Lord, we eat an invisible loaf, given each day in pieces no larger than our need; the broken bread of thy glory shining in the common thing; the broken bread of thy truth nurturing the small words of our lips; the broken bread of thy given life sanctifying the deeds and dreams of love and labor; the broken bread of thy humiliation purging us of pride and pretense; the broken bread of thy joy glimmering in all the beauty and wonder of the broken lights of eternity through days and nights, through flowers and stars, through age and infancy, through mercy and faith. With such broken bread we come to the table of him whose life was broken that ours might be mended, to shine at last with his spirit in the doing of thy will on earth where all things are incomplete until thy blessing rests upon them and they are as they were in heaven. Amen.[1]

Silent Prayer

Sharing of the Cup

> After the same manner also he took the cup, when he had supped, saying, This cup is the new testament in my blood: this do ye, as oft as ye drink it, in remembrance of me. For as often as ye eat this bread, and drink this cup, ye do shew the Lord's death till he come.

[1] Samuel H. Miller.

9

O Christ, who hast given unto thy disciples, here assembled in thy name, this cup as a remembrance that thy life was broken in love for the ransom of many: help us to discern herein thy covenant, putting thy laws into our minds and writing them in our hearts, pledging also to be our Lord and accepting us as thy children. Amen.

Hymn: "Blest be the tie that binds"

Closing Prayer

The grace of the Lord Jesus Christ, and the love of God, and the communion of the Holy Ghost, be with you all.   Amen.

C. A SCRIPTURAL SERVICE

5 Organ Prelude

Opening Hymn

Call to Worship

> The hour cometh, and now is, when the true worshippers shall worship the Father in spirit and in truth: for the Father seeketh such to worship him. God is a Spirit: and they that worship him must worship him in spirit and in truth.

Invocation

> Father of all, who hast brought us thy children through the darkness of night to the light of the morning, bring us now into thy presence. Remove far from us this hour all the clamor and fret of the world. Reveal to us in the quietness of our hearts something of thy beauty, thy truth, and thy love. Make us aware of our fellowship with thee and with one another. Quicken our dull hearts with thy lifegiving Spirit and accept our worship as we say—

The Lord's Prayer

Scripture Lesson—John 6:4-14

Hymn

Words of Institution

> The disciples did as Jesus had appointed them and they made ready the Passover. (*Let the deacons make ready.*) Now when the even hour was come, he sat down with the twelve. And as they did eat, he said, Verily I say unto you, that one of you shall betray me. And they were exceeding sorrowful and began everyone of them to say unto him, Lord, is it I?
>
> (*Pause for self-examination.*)
>
> And as they were eating, Jesus took bread, and blessed it, and brake it (*here the minister may break the bread*), and gave it to the disciples and said, Take, eat, this is my body.
>
> (*Here the bread is distributed.*)
>
> And he took the cup, and gave thanks and gave it to them saying,

Drink ye all of it; for this is my blood of the new covenant, which is shed for many for the remission of sins.

(*Here the cups are distributed.*)

This do, as oft as ye shall drink it, in remembrance of me.

Prayer of Access and Thanksgiving

Almighty God, who by the gift of thy Son hast consecrated for us a new and better way of life, cleanse the thoughts of our hearts by the inspiration of thy Holy Spirit, that, drawing near unto thee with a pure heart we may receive these thy gifts without sin, and worthily magnify thy holy name. And we humbly beseech thee, Father of all mercies and God of all comfort, to grant us thy presence and so sanctify these elements both of bread and wine, and to bless thine own ordinance, that we may receive by faith Christ crucified in us and that he may be one with us and we with him, through Jesus Christ our Lord.

Silent Prayer

A Prayer of Intercession

These words spake Jesus, and lifted up his eyes to heaven and said, Father, the hour has come; glorify thy Son, that thy Son also may glorify thee. I have manifested thy name unto the men which thou gavest me out of the world. I pray for them. I pray not for the world, but for them which thou hast given me; for they are thine and I am glorified in them.

Let us remember the saints and prophets, known and unknown: neither pray I for these alone, but for them also which believe in me through their word.

Let us remember before God, our friends, our parents, those who seek after God, and all those for whom we ought to pray: that they may all be one, as thou, Father, art in me and I in thee, that they also may be one in us.

Let us remember the fellowship of the Kingdom of God into which we are called. Let us remember also our church and our nation of which we are members: that the world may know that thou hast sent me.

Let us remember before God all those whose vision of him is clouded by self, by wealth or poverty, by sickness and pain, by our sins and failings.

(*Brief silence ending with this prayer:*)

For this cause we bow our knees unto the Father from whom all fatherhood in heaven and earth is named, that he would grant us according to the riches of his glory, that we may be strengthened with power through his spirit in the inward man; that Christ may dwell in our hearts through faith; to the end that we, being rooted and grounded in love may be strong to apprehend with all the saints what is the breadth and length and height and depth and to know the love of Christ which passeth knowledge, that we may be filled unto all the fullness of God.

Now unto him that is able to do exceeding abundantly above all that we ask or think, according to the power that worketh in us unto him be glory in the church and in Christ Jesus unto all generations forever and ever.   Amen.

Hymn *or* Anthem

Benediction

Peace I leave with you; my peace I give unto you; not as the world giveth give I unto you. Let not your heart be troubled, neither let it be afraid. Go in peace.   Amen.

Organ Postlude*

Thomas L. Harris

D. A CANDLELIGHT SERVICE

6   An Act of Reverence

Prelude
Lighting of the Candles
Processional Hymn
Introit
Choral Call to Silent Prayer ("The Lord is in his holy temple")
Silent Prayer

An Act of Fellowship

Musical Interlude
Scripture Lesson
Hymn
Communion Sermon *or* Meditation

An Act of Dedication

Hymn of Devotion
Pastoral Prayer
Offertory Sentences
Offertory Music
Presentation of the Offerings

An Act of Renewal

Introductory Sentences to the Communion
Words of Institution and Communion Prayers
The Lord's Prayer
Partaking of the Elements
Concluding Sentences to the Communion
After-Communion Praise in Anthem or Hymn
Benediction
Recessional Hymn
Postlude   *G. Edwin Osborn*

E. A SERVICE FOR A SUMMER CONFERENCE

7   Period of silent meditation

Call to worship—Psalm 121

Hymn: "God, who touchest earth with beauty"

Opening Prayer

> Our Father, thou dost speak to us through the eloquent simplicity and pervasive beauty of thy world. The heavens declare thy glory. The hills assure us that our help comes from thee. By the still waters our souls are restored. At this time of quiet worship, speak, we pray thee, to each of us through thy Son, our Lord and Savior. May we share his peace which passeth all understanding, and may we know the mind of Christ as we recall his words of fellowship here at the table to which in love he has called us.   Amen.

Scripture Lesson—Colossians 3:1-17

Meditation *or reading of one or more appropriate poems in Part IV*

Hymn: "Jesus, thou joy of loving hearts"

Words of Institution—Luke 22:14-20

Partaking of the Elements

Hymn: "Fairest Lord Jesus"

Benediction

> Now unto him that is able to keep you from falling, and to present you faultless before the presence of his glory with exceeding joy, to the only wise God our Saviour, be glory and majesty, dominion and power, both now and ever.   Amen.

F. A SERVICE FOR THE SICK AND SHUT-IN

8 *Let the minister give the invitation in these words:*

Beloved in the Lord, hear what gracious words our Savior Christ saith unto all who truly turn to him: Come unto me, all ye that labor and are heavy-laden, and I will give you rest. Take my yoke upon you, and learn of me; for I am meek and lowly in heart; and ye shall find rest unto your souls. I am the bread of life: he that cometh to me shall never hunger; and he that believeth on me shall never thirst. Him that cometh to me I will in no wise cast out.

Then the minister shall say:

Let us reverently attend to the words of the institution of the holy supper of our Lord Jesus Christ, as they are delivered by the Apostle Paul: I have received of the Lord that which also I delivered unto you, that the Lord Jesus the same night in which he was betrayed took bread: and when he had given thanks, he brake it, and said, Take, eat: this is my body, which is broken for you: this do in remembrance of me. After the same manner also he took the cup, when he had supped, saying, This cup is the new covenant in my blood: this do ye, as oft as ye drink it, in remembrance of me. For as often as ye eat this bread, and drink this cup, ye do show the Lord's death till he come.

And now, in his name, I take these elements to be set apart by prayer and thanksgiving to the holy use for which he has appointed them.

Then the minister shall say:

Let us pray.

Most gracious God, the Father of our Lord Jesus Christ, whose once offering up of himself upon the cross we commemorate before thee: we earnestly desire thy Fatherly goodness to accept this our sacrifice of praise and thanksgiving.

And we pray thee to bless and sanctify with thy Word and Spirit these thine own gifts of bread and wine which we set before thee, that we may receive by faith Christ crucified for us, and so feed upon him that he may be made one with us and we with him.

And here we offer and present unto thee ourselves, our souls and bodies, to be a reasonable, holy, and living sacrifice; and we beseech thee mercifully to accept this our sacrifice of praise and thanksgiving, as, in fellowship with all the faithful in heaven and on earth, we pray thee to fulfill in us, and in all men, the purpose of thy redeeming love.

Through Jesus Christ our Lord; to whom, with thee and the Holy Spirit, be the glory and the praise, both now and evermore.   Amen.

The bread and wine being thus set apart by prayer and thanksgiving, the minister shall say:

The Lord Jesus took bread,

(*Here he shall take some of the bread into his hands*)

And when he had blessed it, he broke it,

(*Here he shall break the bread*)

And gave it to his disciples, as I, ministering in his name, give this bread to you: saying, Take, eat; this is my body, broken for you: this do in remembrance of me.

(*Then the minister, who is himself to communicate, is to administer the bread.*)

Then the minister shall say:

After the same manner our Savior took the cup,

(*Here he shall raise the cup*)

And, having given thanks, as hath been done in his name, he gave it to his disciples; saying, This cup is the new covenant in my blood. Drink ye, all, of it.

(*Then the minister, who is himself to communicate, is to administer the cup.*)

Then the minister shall say:

Let us pray.

We thank thee, O God, for thy great mercy given to us in this sacrament, whereby we are made partakers of Christ. So enrich us by the Holy Spirit that the life of Jesus may be made manifest in us, and the remainder of our days may be spent in thy love and service.

O Lord, holy Father, by whose lovingkindness our souls and bodies are renewed: mercifully look upon this thy servant, that, every cause of sickness being removed, *he* may be restored to soundness of health; through Jesus Christ our Lord.   Amen.

Benediction:

The peace of God, which passeth all understanding, keep your hearts and minds in the knowledge and love of God, and of his Son, Jesus Christ our Lord; and the blessing of God Almighty, the Father, the Son, and the Holy Spirit, be upon you, and remain with you always.   Amen.

The Book of Common Worship

G. COMMUNION SCRIPTURES

1. PRIMARY REFERENCES

Matthew 26:26-29
Mark 14:22-25
Luke 22:14-20
John 6:51-58
1 Corinthians 11:17-34

2. SECONDARY REFERENCES

Luke 24:30, 35
Acts 1:13
Acts 2:42, 46-47
Acts 20:7, 11
Acts 27:35
1 Corinthians 5:7
1 Corinthians 10:1-4, 16-22
1 Corinthians 12:11-13
Hebrews 13:10
2 Peter 2:13
1 John 5:6, 8
Jude 12
Revelation 19:7, 9

H. CALLS TO WORSHIP AND
OPENING SENTENCES

9 Behold, I stand at the door, and knock: if any man hear my voice, and open the door, I will come in to him, and will sup with him, and he with me.

Revelation 3:20

10 Christ our passover is sacrificed for us: therefore let us keep the feast, not with old leaven, neither with the leaven of malice and wickedness; but with the unleavened bread of sincerity and truth.

1 Corinthians 5:7-8

11 We have a great high priest, that is passed into the heavens, Jesus the Son of God. . . . Let us therefore come boldly unto the throne of grace, that we may obtain mercy, and find grace to help in time of need.

Hebrews 4:14, 16

12 If we walk in the light, as he is in the light, we have fellowship one with another, and the blood of Jesus Christ his Son cleanseth us from all sin.

1 John 1:7

13 The mercy of the Lord is from everlasting to everlasting upon them that fear him, and his righteousness unto children's children; to such as keep his covenant, and to those that remember his commandments to do them.

Psalm 103:17-18

14 Beloved, let us love one another: for love is of God; and every one that loveth is born of God, and knoweth God. In this was manifested the love of God toward us, because that God sent his only begotten Son into the world, that we might live through him.

1 John 4:7, 9

15 A new commandment I give unto you, That ye love one another; as I have loved you, that ye also love one another. By this shall all men know that ye are my disciples, if ye have love one to another.

John 13:34-35

16 Whosoever drinketh of the water that I shall give him shall never thirst; but the water that I shall give him shall be in him a well of water springing up into everlasting life.

John 4:14

17 Thus saith the high and lofty One that inhabiteth eternity, whose name is Holy; I dwell in the high and holy place, with him also that is of a contrite and humble spirit, to revive the spirit of the humble, and to revive the heart of the contrite ones.

Isaiah 57:15

18 I the Lord have called thee in righteousness, and will hold thine hand, and will keep thee, and give thee for a covenant of the people, for a light of the Gentiles.

Isaiah 42:6

19 Eye hath not seen, nor ear heard, neither have entered into the heart of man, the things which God hath prepared for them that love him. But God hath revealed them unto us by his Spirit: for the Spirit searchest all things, yea, the deep things of God.

1 Corinthians 2:9-10

20 Blessed are the undefiled in the way, who walk in the law of the Lord. Blessed are they that keep his testimonies, and that seek him with the whole heart. Blessed are they which do hunger and thirst after righteousness: for they shall be filled.

Psalm 119:1-2; Matthew 5:6

21 O give thanks unto the Lord, for he is good: for his mercy endureth for ever. Let the redeemed of the Lord say so, whom he hath redeemed. . . . Hungry and thirsty, their soul fainted in them. Then they cried unto the Lord . . . and he delivered them . . . and he led them forth by the right way. . . . Oh that men would praise the Lord for his goodness, and for his wonderful works to the children of men!

Psalm 107:1-2, 5-8

22 The Lord is nigh unto all them that call upon him, to all that call upon him in truth. He will fulfil the desire of them that fear him: he also will hear their cry, and will save them.

Psalm 145:18-19

23 I will bless the Lord at all times: his praise shall continually be in my mouth. My soul shall make her boast in the Lord: the humble shall hear thereof, and be glad. O magnify the Lord with me, and let us exalt his name together.

Psalm 34:1-3

24 If my people, which are called by my name, shall humble themselves, and pray, and seek my face, and turn from their wicked ways; then will I hear from heaven, and will forgive their sin, and will heal [them].

2 Chronicles 7:14

25 Surely the Lord is in this place. . . . This is none other but the house of God, and this is the gate of heaven.

Genesis 28:16-17

I. INVOCATIONS AND OPENING PRAYERS

26   Our Father, who hast called us into the fellowship of thy Son: draw us closer to thee in this hour of meditation and communion. May our hearts be open to every holy affection and our minds ready to receive and cherish every sacred truth and serious impression. Enlarge our vision, deepen our loyalty, increase our faith, and enrich us anew with thine own divine love. Amen.

Herman Paul Guhsé

27   Almighty and most gracious Father, who this day hast given thy servants to remember the Lord Jesus in the sacrament of the supper: grant that the mind which was in him may also be so formed in us that we may take upon us the burdens and duties which have been appointed us and follow in his steps, bearing contradiction patiently, subduing in ourselves every lawless and guilty desire, setting ourselves steadfastly against every evil work, and by our willing services and sacrifices bringing comfort and hope to those who are distressed. Amen.

Hugh Cameron

28   Father of our spirits, God of love, we pray that in Christ and his cross, we may have communion with thee. In the face of Christ we behold thy glory, and the cross has revealed thee to us. Thou has redeemed us, and called us by name, and we are thine. Make us perfect with thy perfection; holy as thou art holy; merciful as thou art merciful; thine in character as we are thine in right. Amen.

John Hunter

29   Grant, O God, that because we meet together here this morning, life may grow greater for some who have contempt for it, simpler for some who are confused by it, happier for some who are tasting the bitterness of it, safer for some who are feeling the peril of it, more friendly for some who are feeling the loneliness of it, serener for some who are throbbing with the fever of it, holier for some to whom life has lost all dignity, beauty and meaning. Amen.

30   O God, who by the life and death and rising again of thy dear Son hast consecrated for us a new and living way into the holiest of all: cleanse our minds, we beseech thee, by the inspiration of thy Holy Spirit, that drawing near unto thee with a pure heart and conscience undefiled, we may receive these gifts without sin, and worthily magnify thy holy name. Amen.

Liturgy of St. James

31   O God, Creator of the world, Father of mankind: we thank thee for the blessing of life, for the joy of being thy sons. Inspire us, we pray thee, to faithful service in thy family on earth, make us to know the infinite debt we owe our fellowmen, and let no pride of circumstance or narrowness of mind keep us from full and free communion with our brethren. And this we ask through the merits of him who called himself the Son of Man, Jesus Christ, our Lord. Amen.

H. S. Nash

32   Our Father, we thank thee for all the friendly folk who have come into our life this day, gladdening us by their human kindness, and we send them now our . . . thoughts of love through thee. We bless thee that we are set amidst this rich brotherhood of kindred life with its mysterious power to quicken and uplift. Make us eager to pay the due price for what we get by putting forth our own life in wholesome good will and by bearing cheerily the troubles that go with all joys. Above all we thank thee for those who share our higher life, the comrades of our better self, in whose companionship we break the mystic bread of life and feel the glow of thy wonderful presence. Into thy keeping we commit our friends, and pray that we may never lose their love by losing thee. Amen.

Walter Rauschenbusch

33   Our Lord Jesus Christ, who wast dead and art alive forevermore: abide with us as thou didst abide with the disciples who walked with thee along the Emmaus road, and grant that our eyes may be opened and that thou mayest become known to us even as unto them in the breaking of bread. Communing with one another and with thee, may we feel our hearts burn within us, until all good and true and holy things are lovely to us, and we find nothing to fear but that which is hateful in thine eyes. Let thy peace possess our souls, inspire us with thy love, and lift us above all that is selfish and unworthy, until, at last, our spirits gain a perfect victory, and life everlasting. Amen.

James Dalton Morrison

34 O God, the true light of faithful souls, the help of those that flee unto thee, the hope of those who cry unto thee: cleanse us from our sins and from every thought displeasing to thy goodness, that with a pure heart and a clear soul, with calm trust and perfect love, we may worship thee as we seek at this time through these sacred symbols to remember and realize thy love in Jesus Christ our Lord. Amen.

John Hunter

35 We come not into thy presence, most holy Lord God, trusting in our own righteousness but in thy manifold and abiding mercies. Remembering this day the great heart and passion of a son of man of long ago, we are ashamed of our selfish and imperfect lives. We would here be turned to the way of his brave and tender Spirit, and find that wholeness of life which shall be at once a divine blessing for us and a divine ministry from us. Forgive our failures and shortcomings, and by thy grace strengthen our weak desires for goodness, that we may henceforth serve thee without fear and without shame, all the days of our lives. Amen.

Services of Religion

36 O living Christ, make us conscious now of thy healing nearness. Touch our eyes that we may see thee; open our ears that we may hear thy voice; enter our hearts that we may know thy love. Overshadow our souls and bodies with thy presence, that we may partake of thy strength, thy love and thy healing life. Amen.

Robert B. H. Bell

37 Fix, we beseech thee, O bounteous Lord, our eyes and adoration on that open hand which graciously gives us our daily bread. Grant that the wonderful feast of thy Son's body and blood may duly sanctify our tastes to all thy other bounties that we may only relish and continually feed upon thy dear love to us. Amen.*

John Austin

J. BENEDICTIONS AND CLOSING PRAYERS

38 Now the God of peace, that brought again from the dead our Lord Jesus, that great shepherd of the sheep, through the blood of the everlasting covenant, make you perfect in every good work to do his will, working in you that which is well-pleasing in his sight, through Jesus Christ; to whom be glory for ever and ever. Amen.

Hebrews 13:20-21

39 Grace be to you and peace from God the Father, and from our Lord Jesus Christ, who gave himself for our sins, that he might deliver us from this present evil world, according to the will of God and our Father: to whom be glory for ever and ever. Amen.

Galatians 1:3-5

40 Now unto him that is able to do exceeding abundantly above all that we ask or think, according to the power that worketh in us, unto him be glory in the church by Christ Jesus throughout all ages, world without end. Amen.

Ephesians 3:20-21

41 The grace of the Lord Jesus Christ, and the love of God, and the communion of the Holy Ghost, be with you all. Amen.

2 Corinthians 13:14

42 Now unto him that is able to keep you from falling, and to present you faultless before the presence of his glory with exceeding joy, to the only wise God our Saviour, be glory and majesty, dominion and power, both now and ever. Amen.

Jude 24-25

43 Now the God of patience and consolation grant you to be like-minded one toward another according to Christ Jesus: that ye may with one mind and one mouth glorify God, even the Father of our Lord Jesus Christ. Amen.   *Romans 15:5-6*

44 The Lord bless thee, and keep thee: the Lord make his face shine upon thee, and be gracious unto thee: the Lord lift up his countenance upon thee, and give thee peace. Amen.

Numbers 6:24-26

45 Blessing, and glory, and wisdom, and thanksgiving, and honour, and power, and might, be unto our God for ever and ever. Amen.

Revelation 7:12

46 And the peace of God, which passeth all understanding, shall keep your hearts and minds through Christ Jesus. Amen.

Philippians 4:7

K. COMMUNION MUSIC

1. Hymns

An asterisk (*) indicates those hymns which are included in "A Treasury of Communion Poetry" (section IV).

GENERAL HYMNS

* According to thy gracious Word, James Montgomery (John B. Dykes)
* Amidst us our Beloved stands, Charles H. Spurgeon (Lowell Mason)
  And now, O Father, mindful of the love, William Bright (William H. Monk)
  Be still, my soul, for God is near, William Dalrymple Maclagan (Georg Joseph)
  Blest feast of love divine, Edward Denny (George F. Handel)
  Bread of heaven, on thee we feed, Joseph Conder (Richard Redhead)
* Break thou the bread of life, Mary A. Lathbury (William F. Sherwin)
  By Christ redeemed, in Christ restored, George Rawson (Frederick C. Maker or Arthur Sullivan)
  Draw nigh and take the body of your Lord, John Mason Neale, tr. (Arthur Sullivan)
  Here at thy table, Lord, May P. Hoyt (William F. Sherwin)
  Here at thy table, Lord, Samuel Stennett (Hugh Wilson)
* Here, O my Lord, I see thee face to face, Horatius Bonar (Felix Mendelssohn)
  Here, Saviour, we would come, Author unknown (Robert Jackson)
  Jesus, thou joy of loving hearts, Author unknown (Henry Baker)
  Lord, at thy table we behold, Joseph Stennett (Lowell Mason)
  Lord, enthroned in heavenly splendor, George H. Bourne (William Owen)
* Not worthy, Lord, to gather up the crumbs, Edward H. Bickersteth (F. C. Atkinson)
  O bread to pilgrims given, Ray Palmer, tr. (John B. Dykes)
  O Living Bread from heaven, Johann Rist (Samuel S. Wesley)
  Shepherd of souls, refresh and bless, James Montgomery (John B. Dykes)
  The King of love my shepherd is, Henry Williams Baker (John B. Dykes)

Thee we adore, O hidden Saviour, Thomas Aquinas (Composer unknown)

While in sweet communion feeding, Edward Denny (Edward J. Hopkins)

ADVENT

Jesus spreads his banner o'er us, Roswell Park (François H. Barthélémon)

Let all mortal flesh keep silence, Gerard Moultrie (Composer unknown)

Lord of our highest love, G. Y. Tickle (W. H. Havergal)

Now, my tongue, the mystery telling, Thomas Aquinas (*Oxford Hymn Book*)

BROTHERHOOD AND MISSIONS

A holy air is breathing round, Abiel Abbot Livermore (Hans G. Nägeli)

* Beneath the forms of outward rite, James A. Blaisdell (William Gardiner)

Beneath the shadow of the cross, Samuel Longfellow (John B. Dykes)

Blest be the tie that binds, John Fawcett (Hans G. Nägeli)

In memory of the Saviour's love, Thomas Cotterill (Johann M. Haydn)

Lord Jesus Christ, we humbly pray, Henry E. Jacobs (Ignaz J. Pleyel)

THE CHURCH

I love thy Kingdom, Lord, Timothy Dwight (Aaron Williams)

The King of heaven his table spreads, Philip Doddridge (*Scottish Psalter*)

* Thou who at thy first eucharist didst pray, William H. Turton (Charles H. Lloyd)

We build a sanctuary sure, Harold Humber (R. Vaughan Williams)

LENT

* Bread of the world in mercy broken, Reginald Heber (John S. B. Hodges)

Jesus, to thy table led, R. H. Baynes (Arthur Sullivan)

* Let thy blood in mercy poured, John Brownlie (William Benbow)

O Christ, thou gift of love divine, Charles H. Harmer (Charles H. Harmer)

'Tis midnight, and on Olive's brow, William B. Tappan (William B. Bradbury)

'Twas on that night when doomed to know, John Morrison (Edward Miller)

NEW YEAR

From the table now retiring, John Rowe (Isaac B. Woodbury)

O God, unseen, yet ever near, Edward Osler (William Gardiner)

THANKSGIVING

For the bread which thou hast broken, Louis F. Benson (Charles J. Dickinson)

2. Anthems
(SATB unless otherwise indicated)

Agnus Dei, Kalinnikoff-Hollis (Choral Press)

The Apostles' Creed, Genuchi (Ludwig Music Publishing Company)

Behold, What Manner of Love, Paris (R. L. Huntzinger, Inc.)

Bless the Lord, O My Soul, Fearis (Willis Music Company)

Blessed Word of God, Pearsall (B. F. Wood Music Company)

Break Thou the Bread of Life, Sherwin-Lockwood (Southern Music Company)

Come, Holy Spirit (alto solo), Flagler (R. L. Huntzinger, Inc.)

Create in Me a Clean Heart (a cappella), Wilson (Mills Music, Inc.)

God So Loved the World (from The Crucifixion), Stainer (B. F. Wood Music Company)

He Was Crucified, Lotti-Pooler (Augsburg Publishing House)

I Am the Vine (soprano and tenor solos), James (R. L. Huntzinger, Inc.)

I See His Blood upon the Rose, Sateren (Augsburg Publishing House)

I Will Bless the Lord (a cappella), Bortniansky (E. C. Schirmer Music Company)

In Holy Garb Thyself Array (a cappella), Lundquist (Willis Music Company)

Jesus, in Thy Dying Woes, Sateren (Augsburg Publishing House)

Jesus Once for Our Salvation (Christus factus est), Anerio-Manney (B. F. Wood Music Company)

Jesus, the Very Thought of Thee (*Jesu, dulcis memoria*) (*a cappella*), Rheinberger-Bedell (Mills Music, Inc.)

Jesus, Word of God Incarnate (*Ave verum*), Mozart (B. F. Wood Music Company)

Keep Me Ever Close to Thee (SSA and SATB), York (Edward B. Marks Music Corporation)

Let Us Break Bread Together, Spiritual-Sateren (Augsburg Publishing House)

May We Be Wholly Thine, Haynie (Mills Music, Inc.)

Now, My Tongue, the Mystery Telling (*Pange lingua*) (SATTB), Aichinger-Williams (E. C. Schirmer Music Company)

O Hidden Savior, Gregorian Chant-Sateren (Augsburg Publishing House)

O How Plentiful Is Thy Goodness, Flagler (R. L. Huntzinger, Inc.)

O Sacred Head, Hassler Christiansen (Augsburg Publishing House)

O Taste and See, Bortniansky-Williams (E. C. Schirmer Music company)

O Thou Who Camest, Schein-Bach-Bren (Choral Press)

Of the Glorious Body Telling, Vittoria (B. F. Wood Music Company) and Vittoria-Sateren (Augsburg Publishing House)

Quest for God (*a cappella*), Rhea (Ludwig Music Publishing Company)

Soft Were Your Hands, Dear Jesus, O'Hara-Treharne (R. L. Huntzinger, Inc.)

Take the Body of Christ (*a cappella*), Bachmetiev-Williams (E. C. Schirmer Music Company)

Thee We Adore, Diggle (B. F. Wood Music Company)

Therefore We Before Him Bending, Pearsall (B. F. Wood Music Company) and (SA, TB and SATB), Beobide-Williams (E. C. Schirmer Music Company)

We Adore Thee, O Christ (*Adoramus te, Christe*) (SSA, SSS, TTBB and SATB), Lasso-Williams (E. C. Schirmer Music Company)

Worthy Is the Lamb (*a cappella*), Gallus-Lundquist (Willis Music Company)

3. Organ

Adoro te devote, Titcomb (B. F. Wood Music Company)

Agnus Dei, Bizet-Alphenaar (Edward B. Marks Music Corporation)

Ave verum, Titcomb (B. F. Wood Music Company)

Beautiful Savior, twelfth century melody-Christiansen (Augsburg Publishing House)

Choral Prelude ("Christ Lay in the Bonds of Death"), Bach-Alphenaar (Edward B. Marks Music Corporation)

I Thank Thee, Lord, through Thy Dear Son, Karg-Elert (Edward B. Marks Music Corporation)

Jesus, Joy of Man's Desiring, Bach-Alphenaar (Edward B. Marks Music Corporation)

Lamb of God, German chorale-Christiansen (Augsburg Publishing House)

Lenten Meditation, Joela (Edward B. Marks Music Corporation)

Lord, Hear My Deepest Longing, Karg-Elert (Edward B. Marks Music Corporation)

Lord Jesus Christ, Be Present Now, Karg-Elert (Edward B. Marks Music Corporation)

My Jesus, Who Hast Called Me, Brahms-Alphenaar (Edward B. Marks Music Corporation)

O, Bread of Life, Hokanson (Augsburg Publishing House)

O How Shall I Receive Thee, Teschner-Leupold (Augsburg Publishing House)

O Sacred Head, Hassler-Christiansen (Augsburg Publishing House)

Out of the Depths, Kirchenamt-Leupold (Augsburg Publishing House)

O God, Thou Holy God, Brahms-Alphenaar (Edward B. Marks Music Corporation)

O Lamb of God, Most Holy, Karg-Elert (Edward B. Marks Music Corporation)

Prelude ("Parsifal"), Wagner-Alphenaar (Edward B. Marks Music Corporation)

4. Communion Services

Communion Service, Lotti (E. C. Schirmer Music Company)

Communion Service in A Major, Franck (E. C. Schirmer Music Company)

Communion Service in B Minor, Noble (Arthur P. Schmidt Company)

Communion Service in C Major, Ripollès (E. C. Schirmer Music Company)

Mass of the Holy Spirit, Thompson (E. C. Schirmer Music Company)

Short Communion Service, Arensky (E. C. Schirmer Music Company)

II. A Sheaf of Communion Prayers

A. PASTORAL PRAYERS

47 Grant unto us, Almighty God, that we, communing with one another and with thee, may feel our hearts burn within us, until all pure, and just, and holy, and noble things of God and man may be to us lovely, and we may find nothing to fear but that which is hateful in thine eyes, and nothing worth seeking but that which is lovely and fair therein. Let thy divine brightness and peace possess our souls, so that, fearing neither life nor death, we may look to thy lovingkindness and tender mercy to lift us above that which is low and mean within us, and at last to give the spirit within us the victory, and bring us safe through death into the life everlasting. Amen.

George Dawson

48 Our Father God, in this hushed and hallowed hour of our communion worship, we lift our wistful, waiting hearts to thee. Our presence is our prayer, our need is our plea, our assurance is thy faithfulness. At the foot of the cross our faith looks up to thee. We bless thee that thou dost understand so fully the deepest meaning of that upward look. Is it not just thyself who dost inspire it in all the matchless wonder of redeeming love? Our eyes would not and could not strain after thee unless some wondrous gleam of thine had touched us to a sense of infinite need and longing. Hushed before the face of Christ so glorious and beneath this cross so strange, we cannot rest content with what we are. We repent of all that has made our lives so earth-bound, darkened our sky, enslaved our wills, and left our altar fires untended so that we almost feared to look up to thee lest we should make the dread discovery that we had lost the power to see.

And now on the inner threshold of this blessed sacrament we praise thee that thy light doth not cease to shine when we lose sight of it. "The light shineth in darkness and the darkness is not able to put out the light." Blessed be thou, our Savior Christ, for such quenchless light, such wondrous grace, such matchless love. Kneeling at the cross we wait, humbly invoking thy blessing on the sacred symbols of the holy feast for every hushed and waiting heart. Amen.

P. J. Bisset Falconer

49 Almighty God, Father of all who live, Inspirer of all who labor, Comforter of all who suffer, in thy rest may we remain, feeling that beneath us and around us there is a mystery which no thought of ours may fathom, but which is to us full of friendliness and hope. For out of that deep mystery we have come, as have all whom we have loved and known, all who have made our lives beautiful. And so we take their lives as the revealing of powers that are eternal. Knowing their love, their truth, their heroism, we take heart, for thou from whom they came and in whom they have lived wilt sustain us in our hours of need. Not alone have they come, but from generation to generation there have been these testimonies of life divine—men and women who have lived in the power of an endless life.

All the words which we repeat, all the forms which we use are only symbols of that which is deeper than all else—the life eternal welling up in human lives. And we pray that the quality of this life, its deeper meaning, its higher hope may grow strong even in the hours when we feel most our weakness. So may we join together now and always with the great company upon the earth who are looking not at the things that are seen but at the things which are unseen but eternal, and who feel that even according to our need the power to bear and to do and to enjoy will come to us. Amen.

Samuel M. Crothers

50 Holy Father, thy glory makes the earth a temple and all life a sacrament; in the house of thy presence we lift up our hearts in adoration. O thou whose love is our life, reveal thyself to us as we gather at the table of the Lord, to break the loaf broken for us by a broken hand. Lead us beyond the symbol into the mystery of his grace and truth: may it be a festival of his living presence, as when he broke the bread in the gloaming of the day.

God of the living, we praise thee for the company of those gone before, who by their love and loyalty have left us a legacy of faith and hope. We give thee thanks for the fellowship of those who gather here, our comrades and fellow workers, with whom we share thy mercy and adore thy name. Make us members one of another; unite us in one heart with all who seek thee, in one communion with all who love thee, in one steadfast purpose with all who serve thy holy will in faithfulness and joy.

Bless the lonely of soul with thy nearness, and the wounded of heart with thy healing. Give to the hungry of spirit thyself, his bread, even the hidden manna whereof if he eat he shall hunger no more. O thou who hearest what our words cannot tell, lift our spirits to a loftier melody, that our song on earth may blend with the song of the redeemed. Amen.

Joseph Fort Newton

51 Most high and most merciful God, our heavenly Father, led by Jesus Christ we draw near unto thee. Beneath the shadow of his cross, in the light of his revelation, in the communion of his spirit, in the fellowship of his church, we would meditate and pray. Help us to yield ourselves to the influence of this hour of holy memories and immortal hopes. May our spirits be tender to thy touch. May the appeal of thy love enter our hearts. May the sanctities of our Christian faith be more real to us than the things that are seen and temporal.

We would remember Christ—remember that he has eaten with us the bread and drunk the cup of our life, that he had communion with us in our joy and sorrow, and tasted what it is for a man to die. We would remember the gracious beauty of his life, his obedience unto death, the charity of his cross, and his victory over the world's sin and sorrow. We would remember all that we owe to him—our greater nearness to thee and to one another, our knowledge of thy Fatherhood, and of our human brotherhood, our new and more abounding life, our deeper and more peaceful sense of immortality. Impress and quicken our hearts with the memory of our Master and Savior, till we learn to feel it to be no task to serve him, no hardship to follow him in his obedience, and no burden to carry his cross.

We confess with shame that we often forget our Lord. We forget him in our fear and anxiety, in our distrust and doubt of thee, our heavenly Father. We forget him in our indolence and weariness in thy service, in our unforgivingness and uncharitableness of disposition, in our selfishness and worldliness. Forgive, O God, our forgetfulness. Help us so to enter into the spirit of this service that we may go out into the world better prepared to remember Christ amid the care and strife and sorrow of our common days. Amen.

John Hunter

52 In this hour of memory help us, O Lord, to remember all that it is well to remember and to forget what is better forgotten. We remember the great dreams of youth, when we were unselfish and chivalrous and wanted to go forth and do great things for the world. May these memories summon us again to the heroic and brave and true. We remember when love was young and hope was living and faith was strong. We remember the great and hallowed experiences of earlier days which ought to enrich our lives evermore. We remember the great comrades of the past, princely men and queenly women we have known, strong and radiant spirits whose path crossed ours. We remember the sweet souls which we have known and loved and lost awhile.

We remember the sickness and sorrow which led us near to thee. We remember our unanswered prayers and know that had all been answered as we wished it would have brought leanness to our souls. We remember our failures which were stepping stones to real achievement. We remember the cup that would not pass but instead, angels came to minister to us and we were made strong to drink the cup.

We remember Gethsemane and Pilate's Hall and Golgotha and all those last scenes of the whitest life that was ever lived. May we watch with him this hour, and behold his cross as though we sat by his side. May the greatness of his gentleness so captivate our imaginations as to swing us away from our selfish selves and into his great train. Help us to say with him, "Not my will but thine be done." Amen.

Paul Moore Strayer

53 O most gracious Father, look upon us and enlighten our hearts, we pray thee, as we approach the sacrament to which, in his love, thy dear Son has called us. We come in obedience to his last request, to offer the memorial which his church has presented before thee during all the years since he offered himself for the sins of men. We come to receive his life within us and to plead the life he laid down for us. Cleanse us by thy visitation, that with hearts illumined and consciences undefiled we may approach these holy mysteries, with such reverence and contrition, such faith and purity, such love and devotion, as may bring to us the full power and virtue of the sacrament. May thy Son find in us a mansion prepared for his coming, and so fill us with his grace that we may minister to others even as he ministered, and be Christ-bearers to them even as he comes to us through earthly and material symbols in this sacrament. And grant that as we here receive him beneath the unveiled face, in his eternal and glorious majesty, who now reigns, with thee and the Holy Spirit, one God, world without end. Amen.

Charles Fiske

54 Almighty God, our Father, it is by thy grace that we attain unto holiness, and it is by thy light that we find wisdom. We humbly pray that thy grace and light may be given unto us so that we may come into the liberty of purity and truth. Wilt thou graciously exalt our spirits and enable us to live in heavenly places in Christ Jesus. Impart unto us a deep dissatisfaction with everything that is low, and mean, and unclean, and create within us such pure desire that we may appreciate the things which thou hast prepared for them that love thee. Wilt thou receive us as guests of thy table. Give us the glorious sense of thy presence, and the precious privilege of intimate communion. Feed us with the bread of life; nourish all our spiritual powers; help us to find our delight in such things as please thee. Give us strength to fight the good fight of faith. Give us holy courage, that we may not be daunted by any fear, or turn aside from our appointed task. Make us calm when we have to tread an unfamiliar road, and may thy presence give us companionship divine. Amen.

John Henry Jowett

55 O God, we thank thee for the communion of suffering that is represented here as we partake of the emblems of the sacrificial death of Jesus Christ. Help us to come with a willingness to join the fellowship of those who bear the marks of pain. We thank thee, too, for this as a communion of power, and thinking of what those few men did who supped with Jesus that night, we pray that thou wilt send us out with new ability to labor at his tasks. And we are glad, also, that this is a communion of hope, in which we look forward to sitting down at the Master's table in his kingdom. O, our Lord, let the day of thy triumph come speedily. Amen.

Jack Finegan

56 Most holy and most merciful God, led by Jesus Christ, we draw near to thee. We remember how on the night on which he was betrayed he took bread and brake it, and took the cup and blessed it, as symbols of his outpoured life, of the love of God, and of the bonds which unite man to man. We would catch something of the mystery of the Master's mind and heart, and the message of his hand and eye as he gathered with his disciples in the upper room. Lord God, make us sensitive to the ways by which he would draw us to thyself, and especially of every claim of our fellowman upon us which he has made the more clear. Draw us together in unity of spirit, and with steadfast purpose to his feet.

We thank thee that we can be part of that church which has spread from the upper room to the ends of the earth, and which has passed on the flame of Christ's unrelenting cause. Purify thy church. Bind up its broken body. Center its mind upon things that abide. Bless this and every congregation. And may each of us be faithful to the vows we have made before thee, and go forward from this place to our work among men as those who know whom they serve. Amen.

Elmore McNeill McKee

WORLD COMMUNION SUNDAY

57 Behold us, Lord, people of every race and clime gathered about thy table to share again in the gracious benefits of thy redeeming love. In penitence and faith we await thy pardoning grace. In love and trust we pray for our unity in the fellowship and service of thy dear name.

Pour out, we beseech thee, O Lord, thy Spirit upon thy church, that to all its members may come new visions, new life, new fellowship with Christ, its living bread. Send us out, if thou wilt, and through us send out many another to work for the extension of thy kingdom throughout the world. Open our hearts that we may receive thy power; open our eyes that we may see Christ with hands outstretched to bless. Do with us what thou wilt and as thou wilt. So shall the earth be filled with the knowledge of thyself as the waters cover the sea. And to thee be the glory and praise, now and forever. Amen.

National Council of Churches

FOR MAUNDY THURSDAY

58 Our heavenly Father, very reverently now we would bow before thee, recognizing the great cost of our salvation. We remember how love had to walk the way of agony and sacrifice for our redemption.

Very humbly we would bow before thee, knowing our own unworthiness. Forgive us our fitfulness of faith, our transient moods of spiritual enthusiasm, the faltering way in which we follow. Look upon us with eyes of understanding love.

Wilt thou so draw us to thyself and share with us thy strength, that despite our frailty we may be dependable disciples of our Savior Jesus Christ.

And now on this last night of his life on earth we ask thy special blessing upon our worship. We would remember his agony in the garden. We would remember the heartache and pain. We would take fresh courage in his spiritual triumph. Through these precious elements of his Supper wilt thou teach us to live for him who died for us.

Bless all who are gathered together at this table. Give us deeper understanding and a spiritual awareness because we have this night been together with thee. For we ask these mercies in Christ's name. Amen.

Lowell M. Atkinson

FOR MAUNDY THURSDAY

59 Our heavenly Father, we gather together this night with humble and reverent spirits, awed by the sacredness of this hour. When we think of our Saviour's last night on this earth we thank thee for the quality of his spirit, who, when confronting the darkness and the tragic spectre of death, still could place his all in thy keeping and still could trust completely thy holy will.

We remember his affection for his friends, frail though their faith was, and we would take thought of our own high responsibility and our sacred privilege to be worthy to be among his friends. Grant that we may learn to be faithful, that we may be true and not falter, that we may follow but not afar off.

We thank thee for the joy that is ours of coming together in time of prayer when we may renew our consecration and strengthen our spirits by partaking of the sacred elements. Let thy blessing be upon our worship and especially let thy spirit be felt in our heart, that we may truly have fellowship with our Lord this night.

We thank thee for this Holy Week, for the way our thoughts are directed afresh to thee, for the manner in which our imaginations are kindled as we follow in the steps of the Master through the last week of his earthly life. Wilt thou give to us the secret of his peace, the thrill and wonder of his victory. Teach us to be faithful to him, who has never failed us. Wilt thou chasten and humble us in spirit, and grant that we may feel that our lives are linked the more closely with that of our Savior, because of these sacred times of worship.

Bless our fellowship this night and bless all of the far-reaching fellowship of thy church. Grant that our prayers and our devotion may truly be acceptable in thy sight; through Jesus Christ our Lord. Amen.

Lowell M. Atkinson

AT THE RECEPTION OF NEW MEMBERS

60 Almighty God, the Father of our Lord Jesus Christ, we entreat thee to bestow thy grace upon thy servants who have this day made solemn profession of their faith before thee. Deepen in their hearts the holy impressions of this hour. Continually renew and strengthen their desire and purpose, that they may reverently take into their hands the memorials of their Lord's death, and being greatly strengthened thereby may run with patience the race before them, looking unto Jesus. Do thou make them to be helpers of one another's joy and victory over evil. Alike in their hours of sacramental fellowship and of active service in the world, fill their hearts with the peace which the world cannot take away. Stablish, strengthen, and settle them; and when they have served their generation by the will of God, do thou receive them into the joy of their Lord. Amen.

Charles Carroll Alberston

B. PRAYERS BEFORE THE SUPPER

61 O God, the Searcher of hearts, prepare our hearts to receive the sacrament of Christ's body and blood with true piety and devotion. Pour thy grace into our souls that we may worthily partake of this sacred feast. Give to us penitent hearts, love and charity toward our neighbors, a full purpose to lead a better life, to keep thy commandments and to walk in thy holy ways. May we draw near with faith and may we take this holy sacrament to our comfort and be thereby refreshed in spirit, so that we may rejoice in thee with all our heart. Grant that in all the future course of our lives we may show ourselves such ingrafted members of the body of thy Son that we may never be drawn to do anything that may dishonor his name. Grant all this for his merits and mercy's sake. Amen.

62 O heavenly Father, who dost govern the thoughts of men: bring to our minds the upper room where the Lord Jesus broke the bread with his disciples in the night before he was crucified; grant to us that, being of that company, we may look into the face of him who gave himself for the world. While we eat of his bread and drink of his cup, fill our lives with his life and send us forth to think his thoughts, to say his words, to do his deeds; and so, O Father, grant that, though we may know it not, the light of his face may shine in our faces, and all men may take note that we have been with Jesus, who liveth and reigneth with thee and the Holy Spirit, the God of everlasting love, world without end. Amen.

Charles Lewis Slattery

63 Blessed be thy name, O God of our salvation, for the opportunity thou dost give us of observing the holy sacrament of the Lord's Supper. Prepare us, we beseech thee, for this ordinance. Inspire us with ardent love to the Saviour. Work in us unfeigned sorrow for our sins. Give us sincere and humble purposes of new obedience, that we may with a true heart devote ourselves to his service. And enable us, when we partake of this ordinance, to feed by faith on the blessings represented by it, so as to promote our spiritual nourishment and growth in grace. Help us to walk before thee in the land of the living, seeking our rest in thee, who dealest bountifully with us, and presenting our bodies a living sacrifice, holy and acceptable unto God, which is our reasonable service. Enable us to be steadfast and immovable, always abounding in the work of the Lord; that when our course in this life is ended, we may be admitted to the supper of the Lamb, and may sit down with him in the kingdom of his Father. Amen.

64 We praise and adore the ever blessed Trinity for the redemption of the world by our Lord Jesus Christ, and we come, O blessed Savior, now to take and eat thy body, which was broken for us. We come joyfully to drink of that cup which is the New Testament in thy blood, which blood thou hast shed for the remission of the sins of many. O merciful Jesus, create in us a mighty hunger after this bread of life, this bread which came down from heaven. Let this immortal food instill in our weak and languishing souls new supplies of grace, new life, new love, new vigor and new resolutions. Amen.

65 O almighty God, whose blessed Son did institute and ordain holy mysteries as pledges of his love and for a continual rememberance of his death: mercifully grant that we and all who shall come to this holy table may be filled with a deep sense of the exceeding holiness of that blessed mystery, and, drawing near with true penitent hearts and lively faith, in love and charity with all men, may worthily receive that holy sacrament and obtain the fulness of thy grace, to our present comfort and everlasting salvation. Amen.

66 Lord, we are not worthy that thou shouldest come under our roof; but speak the word only, and thy servants shall be healed. Foxes have holes, and birds of the air have nests; but in our souls the Son of Man hath not a fit place wherein to lay his head. But as thou didst vouchsafe to be laid in the stall and manger of brute beasts; as thou didst not disdain to be received into the house of Simon the leper; as thou didst not reject the woman which was a sinner when she approached and touched thee, nor abhor her lips when she kissed thy feet; neither the thief on the cross when he confessed thee; even so vouchsafe to admit us also, bruised and sinful creatures, to a communion and participation in the holy, quickening, and saving sacrament of thy most blessed body and blood. Amen.

St. Chrysostom

67   O Lord our God, who desireth not the death of a sinner, but that he
should turn from his sin unto thee, and live: we give thee humble
thanks and praise for all that thou hast done for the children of men, for
the great love wherewith thou hast loved us, for the redemption thou hast
wrought for us in Christ, and for the abundant life that is ours through
him. Forgive us, whom thou hast made heirs of God and joint-heirs with
Christ, that we should be so blind to the riches of our inheritance, so
content to be little in spirit, so indifferent to the divine opportunities of
this earthly life. Grant us in this sacrament the vision of thee as thou art,
and of ourselves as thou wouldst have us be, that hating our evil and
careless ways we may look unto thee and be saved. Grant us in this sacrament to know the sufficiency of thy grace and to be partakers of those
joys unspeakable which thou hast promised to them that love thee. Lift
us now into true communion with thee, and so abide with us that we
may walk before thee all our days in the peace of the forgiven, in the joy
of the redeemed, and in the power of the sons of God. Amen.

Ronald H. G. Budge

68   O God, Father of light, Source of life, Author of grace and Founder
of the worlds, Fount of all knowledge, Treasure of all wisdom, In-
stiller of holiness and Teacher of pure prayer, thou kindly Helper of the
soul: thou dost give the weak of soul who trust in thee those things
whereof the angels long to have sight. Thou who hast raised us from the
depths into light, hast given us life out of death, who hast graciously
brought us out of slavery into freedom, has scattered the darkness of sin
by the presence of thine only-begotten Son; even now thyself, Master and
Lord, enlighten the eyes of our understanding by the visitation of thy
Holy Spirit, that we may partake without condemnation of this immortal and heavenly food, and sanctify us through and through in body,
soul and spirit. Amen.

Liturgy of St. Mark

69   Lord Jesus, we desire the heavenly country, and we have forsaken all
that we may seek it. Thou knowest our weakness and weariness, for
thou wast once a man of sorrows, compassed with infirmity and in all
points tempted like as we are. Thou knowest how wide is the wilderness
and how rough the road, for thou hast passed this way before us. We
bless thee that thou hast thought in great compassion of thy poor pilgrims, and hast caused a house to be built and a table to be furnished for
us here. Gladly do we hearken to thy voice which bids us turn aside and

find refreshment for our souls. O satisfy us with the goodness of thy house, that in the strength of this meat we may go forward on our pilgrimage, yea, go from strength to strength until we appear before God in Zion. Amen.

David Smith

70 O Lord and heavenly Father, we thy humble servants earnestly desire thy fatherly goodness, mercifully to accept this our sacrifice of praise and thanksgiving; beseeching thee that, looking unto Christ and entering into the fellowship of his suffering, we may be changed into his likeness and with him pass from death into life. And here we offer and present unto thee, O Lord, ourselves, our souls and bodies, to be a reasonable, holy and living sacrifice unto thee; humbly beseeching thee, that all we who are partakers of this holy communion may be filled with thy grace and heavenly benediction. And although we be unworthy, through our manifold sins, to offer unto thee any sacrifice, yet we beseech thee to accept this our bounden duty and service; not weighing our merits, but pardoning our offences, according to thine abundant mercies in Christ Jesus our Lord; through whom all honor and glory be unto thee, O Father Almighty, world without end. Amen.

71 The world has traveled far, O God, from that night when Jesus broke bread with his disciples, that last night on which he was betrayed. Yet the distance is only one of time, for we in this hour again break bread and take the cup of the new covenant. Again, we are his disciples, waiting for his word of peace. We have not come to this moment in vain, nor listened without reward; to our waiting hearts the everliving message of Christ has spoken. We thank thee for this continuing assurance of thy presence. Thou hast given us the tongue of the disciple that we may know how to speak a word in season to him that is weary. Accept our gratitude for this sacred trust, this holy privilege, and keep us ever faithful to its use. Speak to us and through us, O God, unto the bringing of this will on earth, as it is in heaven. Amen.

Robert E. Keighton

72 O God our Father, before we eat of this bread and drink of this wine, cleanse our hearts and minds of all haste and confusion, lest we know not what we do. Deepen us down to silence that we may let our lives speak out of their own need and for their own glory. When we take this bread in our hand, remind us of him whose body was broken, and do not

let us shun that suffering which still tortures the world in our time. When we lift this wine to our lips, reveal to our thirsting souls the greatness of his spirit whose soul was meek and lowly, and do not let us hide the poverty of our hearts from one another. If there be strength of soul within us, grant, O God, that we will not curse this hour by our shallowness, but meet the gifts of Christ with our whole selves, in his name. Amen.

Samuel H. Miller

73 O Master of life, who didst gather thy disciples round thee in the upper room to give them there the sacrament of thy body and thy blood: take us also, unworthy as we are, into the fellowship of those who would follow thee. We acknowledge our shortcomings and our sins, our inconstant minds and hearts, and our slackness in devotion. But thou dost not forsake us even when we fail thee. Accept us not for what we are, but for what thou canst create in us, O Savior who by thy sacrifice hast sealed us for thine own. Amen.

Walter Russell Bowie

74 O Savior of men, thou didst die for our redemption. But even in the shadow of death thy victory began. We praise thee for the last supper with thy disciples and for its pledge of the kingdom of God to come. We bless thee that still we may eat and drink by faith, and feed on thee in our hearts with thanksgiving. Impart thy very self to all our spirits, O eternal Love, who art alive for evermore.

Give us grace, O Lord, this day to live as those who constantly remember thee. In our daily work or pleasure, in common duty or in special trial, keep thy cross and passion present before our eyes; let thy redeeming love burn in our hearts.

Divide thy cup of salvation among all our friends and kinsfolk. Let not one refuse to taste and see how gracious thou art. We ask it for thy mercy's sake. Amen.

A Book of Family Worship

75 Almighty and most merciful Father, we are about to commemorate the death of thy Son Jesus Christ, our Saviour and Redeemer. Grant, O Lord, that our whole hope and confidence may be in his merits, and thy mercy; enforce and accept our imperfect repentance; make this commemoration available to the confirmation of our faith, the establishment of our hope, and the enlargement of our love, and make the death of thy dear Son Jesus Christ effectual to our redemption. Support us by thy

Holy Spirit throughout our lives, and receive us at last into everlasting happiness. Amen.*

Samuel Johnson

76 O thou great Friend of all the sons of men, the Comrade of the beaten and broken, of the young and old, the valiant and the timid, bring us within the circle of thy love and power and wisdom, that we may be to others what thou art to us, the unfailing Companion, the cup of strength to souls in need, the reconciling Friend. As we sit at thy table and meditate upon thy love for all the world, let our holy communion be in truth within the world-wide community of thy holy church. Draw us closer to thyself and so closer to one another in Jesus Christ thy Son our Savior. Amen.

David A. MacLennan

77 Let us so live tomorrow, that we and others may be conscious where we have lingered today. We come to thee, thy sorrowing, sinning, defeated, careless, struggling, but ever-returning children. May these signs signify not so much thy love as our response to that love. We keep this feast "till he come"; then it, too, shall fade into the memories of earth because of the marriage supper of the Lamb. We accept thine invitation, Lord,—unworthy enough, but not unworthily, because in obedience to thy command and in love to thee. If tomorrow our plans are broken, may we be patient, and, thinking of that Broken Life, may we offer the parts of our broken plans as a sacrament, a sacred thing, to thee. Holy Spirit, take of the things of Christ, and show them to us, and show them through us, that the world may know thee. Amen.

Maltbie D. Babcock

C. PRAYERS AFTER THE SUPPER

78   O Lord of souls, who hast chosen and called us to serve in thy church, all our trust is in thee, for in thee are the springs of our life. Abundantly give us of thy blessed Spirit, without whom nothing is strong, nothing is holy, and use us as it shall please thee for the glory of thy name. Increase our faith, mellow our judgment, stir our zeal, deepen our devotion. Let our lives enforce what our lips utter. Do thou choose for us the work we do and the place in which we do it, the success we win and the harvest we reap. Preserve us from jealousy and impatience; from self-will and depression. Make us faithful unto death and give us at last the crown of life. All this we ask for Christ's sake. Amen.

Family Devotions

79   Grant, O Lord, that the ears which have heard the voice of thy songs may be closed to the voice of clamour and dispute; that the eyes which have seen thy great love may also behold thy blessed hope; that the tongues which have sung thy praise may speak the truth; that the feet which have walked thy courts may walk in the region of light; and that the bodies which have partaken of thy living body may be restored in newness of life. Glory be to thee for thine unspeakable gift. Amen.

Liturgy of Malabar

80   Almighty and everliving God, who hast vouchsafed to regenerate us thy servants by water and the Holy Ghost, and hast given unto us forgiveness of all our sins: strengthen us, we beseech thee, O Lord, with the Holy Ghost the Comforter, and daily increase in us thy manifold gifts of grace: the spirit of wisdom and understanding, the spirit of counsel and heavenly strength, the spirit of knowledge and true godliness; and fill us, O Lord, with the spirit of thy holy fear, now and for ever. Amen.*

Acts of Devotion

81   O God, before whose face the generations rise and pass away: age after age the living seek thee, and find that of thy faithfulness there is no end. Our fathers in their pilgrimage walked by thy guidance, and rested on thy compassion; still to their children be thou the cloud by day, the fire by night. O thou sole Source of peace and righteousness, take now the veil from every heart; and join us in one communion with thy prophets and saints who have trusted in thee, and were not ashamed. Not of our worthiness, but of thy tender mercy, hear our prayer. Amen.*

James Martineau

82   Accomplish thy perfect work in our souls, O Father. Let us become day by day purer, freer, more heavenly, more happy, and preserve us unto eternal life. Bless, animate and sustain us, and raise us mightily above all that would distract us, to thyself and the consciousness of thy fellowship which gives joy to all who dwell therein. As yet we are bound with many chains; we tarry among things seen and temporal, and feel their oppression; we are exposed to the storms of the outer world, and are wrestling with its ills. But we are not dismayed, for we are akin to thee, O spirit of the Lord, and can experience thy heavenly influence. Unite us ever more closely to the company of faithful hearts whom thou art sanctifying and preparing for heaven. Fill us with their faith and love and hope. Amen.

V. R. Reinhard

83   We most earnestly beseech thee, O thou Lover of mankind, to bless all thy people, the flocks of thy fold. Send down into our hearts the peace of heaven, and grant us also the peace of this life. Give life to the souls of all of us, and let no deadly sin prevail against us, or any of thy people. Deliver all who are in trouble, for thou art our God, who settest the captives free; who givest hope to the hopeless, and help to the helpless; who liftest up the fallen; and who art the heaven of the shipwrecked. Give thy pity, pardon and refreshment to every Christian soul, whether in affliction or error. Preserve us, in our pilgrimage through this life, from hurt or danger, and grant that we may end our lives as Christians, well-pleasing to thee and free from sin, and that we may have our portion and lot with all thy saints. Amen.

Liturgy of St. Mark

84   Almighty God, Giver of the seed and of the soil, of the word and the understanding, of the heavenly life and the earthly vessel: teach us the good husbandry of the heart, so that thy precious word may bring forth fruit; and that we, having the conditions of spiritual readiness to receive the water of life, may thereby be refreshed for our daily life, and fitted at last for the life eternal. Amen.

George Dawson

D. LITANIES AND RESPONSIVE PRAYERS

85   *WE GIVE OURSELVES TO THEE*

Almighty God, uncreated Light and Love, we bless and magnify thy holy name. All things come of thee. Earth and heaven are of thy will. All souls are thine. Worthy art thou to receive all glory and praise!
We bless and magnify thy name, O God.

Gracious Father, we thank thee more especially for Jesus Christ our Lord, whose life is our example, whose death is our redemption, and whose rising is the first fruits of our immortality.
We bless thee for thy Son, our Savior, O God.

Giver of all good, help us now to give ourselves to thee, our bodies and souls, a living sacrifice, which is our reasonable service.
May we be worthy children of thine, O God.

Father of the whole family in heaven and earth, purge us of bitterness and deliver us from hate. We would be joined with the need of the whole world. We would be joined with the high company of heaven. May thy will be done in earth as it is in heaven until there is "one fold and one Shepherd."
May we be faithful disciples of thy kingdom, O God.

Lord God Incarnate, we remember Christ according to his word: his lowly way, his truth which does not pass though heaven and earth be shaken, his trust in our blind and wayward nature, his courage unto death, his love unto sacrifice. The remembrance of him quickens into a Presence.
May he be known to us in the breaking of bread, O God.

Thou who art bread and wine, we would feed on thee in the hunger and thirst of our sorrow and pain, our want and weariness, our folly and sin, our yearnings and hope.
Renew our life, O God.

Therefore with angels and archangels we laud and magnify thy holy name, evermore praising thee and saying, Holy, holy, holy, Lord God of hosts. Heaven and earth are full of thy glory.

*Glory be to thee, O Lord most high. Amen.**

George A. Buttrick

86   *MAY WE REMEMBER THEE*

Lord, if we have forgotten thee in the distractions of the workaday world and lost the sense of thy presence in the crowded hours of our days:

May we remember thee, O Lord.

If we have forsaken thine altars and turned our hearts from worship and our lips from praise:

May we remember thee, O Lord.

If we have withheld more than is meet and kept for ourselves what we should have given away:

May we remember thee, O Lord.

If thy service has made demands upon us which we have been slow to grant and the tasks of thy kingdom have found us reluctant to assume them:

May we remember thee, O Lord.

If we have looked only upon our own things and not upon the things of others and so shortened our vision that we could not see the white fields of the world ready to harvest:

May we remember thee, O Lord.

O Lord, as we sit together in the gracious fellowship of this communion hour, with hearts that are one in aspiration and in hope, help us to recall that thou hast said:

This do in remembrance of me.

As we search our hearts, that we may worthily partake of these emblems of the eternal love, hallowed by the devotion of the ages, may we with one accord accept the Master's commandment:

This do in remembrance of me.

James Dalton Morrison

87   *FOR THIS HOUR OF REMEMBRANCE*

O Lord, our gracious Father, who keepest truth to a thousand generations, and forgivest iniquity and transgression and sin: look on us in love and pity as we gather before thee now, a company of sinful people, needy and weak, who require thy help, and often reject it.

O Lord, look upon us in love as we gather at thy table.

Draw near to us, we beseech thee, that we may draw near to thee, and show us something of the sweetness and blessedness of thy fellowship and love, that our sluggish desires may be kindled to long for more of that which is our only satisfying good, even thy presence, and the common assurance that thou art our friend.

O Lord, draw near to us in this hour of remembrance.

O Lord, look upon us, we beseech thee, as we are gathered here before thee, and give us some quickening and glad sense of thy friendship and thy power, that we may walk in the light, howsoever we have brought our darkness to it. Scatter thou all thoughts and desires, all anxieties and perplexities, all solicitations of earthly good which may come between us and thee. And help us, with all our hearts, with all our souls, and strength, and minds, to yield ourselves unto thee, and to enter into the communion and blessedness of this hour of prayer.

O Lord, give us some quickening sense of thy friendship and power.

We thank thee for all the helps we find, even in outward things. We bless thee that the associations of this day, and the memories of this place, and the companionship of each other, can help us to draw near to thee.

O Lord, make thyself known to us in the breaking of bread.

To this end, O Lord, help and bless us in our worship, and shed abroad upon each heart waiting before thee the needful gifts and graces, that all of us may indeed have our fellowship with the Father and with the Son Jesus Christ.

O Lord, evermore would we seek thee in the fellowship of bread and wine. Amen.

Alexander Maclaren

88 *AN EMMAUS LITANY*

By the love with which thou didst draw near to thy disciples as they went to Emmaus and talked together of thy passion, draw near and join thyself to us who reason of holy things, and give us, as we can bear it, the knowledge of mysteries.

Hear us, blessed Jesus.

By the mercy with which at first their eyes were holden that they should not know thee, be merciful to those who are slow of heart to believe.

Hear us, blessed Jesus.

By the compassion with which, amid the joy of thy resurrection, thou didst seek them out who were sad, console the fainthearted who have not yet learned to rejoice in thee.

Hear us, blessed Jesus.

By the humility with which thou didst will to appear ignorant of thine own great mysteries, suffering thy disciples to tell thee concerning thyself, win wholly to thyself the hearts and minds of those who are weak in faith.

Hear us, blessed Jesus.

By the patience with which, beginning at Moses, thou didst expound unto them in all scriptures the things concerning thyself, open thou the understanding of those who do not yet love thy written Word.

Hear us, blessed Jesus.

By the fire with which thou didst make their hearts to burn within them, as thou didst talk with them by the way, opening to them the scriptures, inflame with devotion every heart that is not already burning with the love of thee, and consume with zeal those that thou hast kindled.

Hear us, blessed Jesus.

By the wisdom with which thou didst make as though thou wouldst have gone further, thus inviting them to constrain thee to tarry with them, may no soul whom thou desirest to bless suffer thee to depart until it has received from thee the blessing which thou art waiting to give.

Hear us, blessed Jesus.

By the charity with which thou didst go in and tarry with thy disciples when the day was far spent, fulfil in every soul that loveth thee that word of thine which said, I will come in to him and will sup with him, and he with me.

Hear us, blessed Jesus.

By the blessing wherewith thou didst manifest thyself to thy disciples in the breaking of bread, let every act of thine, whether of nature or of grace, be to us a sacrament, opening the eyes of our faith that we may know thee.

Hear us, blessed Jesus.

By the power whereby thou didst vanish out of their sight that their faith in the mystery of thy resurrection might be increased, strengthen and confirm this faith in us.

*Hear us, blessed Jesus. Amen.**

Devotional Offices for General Use

89 *PETITION FOR THE CHURCH*

For the church of Jesus Christ, that sacred mystery; for the benediction of her presence in the world; for her growth throughout the ages; for all faithful souls who have served her; for all martyrs who have died for her; for all saints who have glorified her; for all prophets who have chastened and corrected her; for all priests and ministers who have taught and led her; for the inspiration of her worship, the grace of her sacraments, the help of her discipline, the joy of her fellowship, and for all the blessings that are ours because of her:

We praise thee, O God.

Wherein we, members of Christ's holy church, have proved faithless to our trust, have broken our vows, have wronged one another, have let bitterness mar our fellowship, have neglected thy little ones, have condoned what is contrary to the Master's spirit, and have compromised with the evils of the world:

Have mercy upon us, O Lord, and forgive us.

Pour thy holy and consecrating Spirit upon us, and upon thy whole church; that repentant and forgiven she may burn with love for God and man; and feeling shame for the evils around her, may she serve thee with all her heart and soul and mind and strength in the work of thy salvation, through Jesus Christ our Lord:

Hear our prayer, O Lord.

Grant to the church a new vision and a new charity, new wisdom and fresh understanding, the revival of her brightness and the renewal of her unity; that the eternal message of thy Son, undefiled by the traditions of men, may be hailed as the good news of salvation from all the ills of the world for all time:

Hear our prayer, O Lord.

Intercession Services

90 *A PRAYER FOR THE WHOLE CHURCH*

For the whole church of Christ, scattered abroad in five continents, and bearing many names, that it may be no longer torn asunder, divided in

itself or weak, but may become a glorious church, without spot or blemish, fulfilling thy perfect will:
Thy will be done in thy church, we beseech thee, O Lord.

For the churches that are passing through times of suffering and persecution, that their faith and courage may not fail nor their love grow cold:
Save them and us, we beseech thee, O Lord.

For the churches that are strong in faith, that they may abound in grace and in knowledge and love of thee:
Use them and us, we beseech thee, O Lord.

For all weak and struggling churches, that they may persevere and be strong, overcoming those forces which hinder their growth or threaten their existence:
Sustain them and us, we beseech thee, O Lord.

For the younger churches of Asia, Africa, and the islands of the sea, that they may grow into the full stature of the completeness of Christ, bringing new treasures into the church of the ages:
Direct their steps and ours, we beseech thee, O Lord.

For the older churches of the east and the west, that they may increase in wisdom and humility and find new ways to make the message of the gospel understood in the world of today:
Renew them and us, we beseech thee, O Lord.

For our brotherhood, that we may hold fast to the truth, be delivered from all error, and walk with one another in the way of love and unity:
Teach us and guide us, we beseech thee, O Lord.

For the several councils of the churches that through them Christians may the sooner overcome their reluctance to cooperate with one another, transcend their differences, and be knit more closely together in a fellowship of understanding and love:
Draw all churches nearer to one another, we beseech thee, O Lord.

O sovereign and almighty God, bless all thy people and all thy flock; give thy peace, thy help, thy love to us thy servants, the sheep of thy fold, that we may be united in the bond of peace, one body and one Spirit, in one hope of our calling, in thy divine and boundless love; for the sake of Jesus Christ, the great Shepherd of the sheep. Amen.*
World Council of Churches

91 *THANKSGIVING FOR THE CHURCH*

For the church of the living God, born of the Spirit:
God be praised.

For the Christ, the Head of the church, the Captain of our salvation:
God be praised.

For the fellowship of the church established in the bonds of faith, transcending barriers of class, country and race:
God be praised.

For all that sustains the membership of the body of Christ in prosperity and adversity:
God be praised.

For the fortitude of those who through the centuries and today, in fidelity to their faith, have endured suffering and persecution, remaining faithful even to death:
God be praised.

For the growing unity of the church, born of a new understanding of our oneness in Christ and in the fellowship of the Spirit:
God be praised.

For the sufficiency of the gospel, for the hope born of Christian faith, for the longing of humankind for peace and good will, and for the reality of the kingdom of heaven:
God be praised.

Now to the King, eternal, immortal, invisible, the only wise God, be honor and glory, forever and ever. Amen.

World Council of Churches

E. CHURCH COVENANTS AND AFFIRMATIONS OF FAITH

A CHURCH COVENANT

Affirming our membership in the holy church throughout all the world, and our fellowship in this congregation with those who have obtained like precious faith, we renew our vows of fidelity to our Lord Jesus Christ, and solemnly covenant and promise:

That we will walk together in brotherly love, as is becoming in members of a Christian church; that we will exercise an affectionate care and watchfulness over each other, and faithfully admonish and entreat one another as occasion may require.

That we will not forsake the assembling of ourselves together, nor neglect to pray for ourselves and others.

That we will endeavor to bring up such as may at any time be under our care, in the nurture and admonition of the Lord, and by a pure and holy example, to win our kindred and acquaintances to the Savior, to holiness, and to eternal life.

That we will rejoice in each other's happiness, and endeavor with tenderness and sympathy to bear each other's burdens and sorrows.

That we will not bring forward to the church a complaint against any member for any personal trespass against us, until we have taken the steps pointed out by Christ in his instructions to his disciples, and that all private offenses which can be privately settled, we will never make public.

That we will live circumspectly in the world, denying ungodliness and worldly lusts, setting a worthy example, and remembering that as we have been voluntarily buried by baptism, and have been raised up from the emblematic grave, so there is on us a special obligation henceforth to lead a new and holy life.

That we will strive together for the support of a faithful evangelical ministry among us; that according to our abilities and opportunities we will, as faithful servants of the Lord, do good to all men, especially in helping to extend the gospel in its purity and power to the whole human family, and that we will regularly support the work of the church by systematic contributions of money.

And that through life, amidst evil report and good report, we will humbly and earnestly seek to live to the glory of him who hath called us out of darkness into his marvelous light.

Hymns of the United Church

93 *A CHURCH COVENANT*

We have been brought by divine grace to receive the Lord Jesus Christ and to give ourselves up to him. We have also acknowledged a special obligation to live a new and holy life, in that we have voluntarily been buried in baptism and raised up from the emblematical grave. And now, relying on the gracious aid of our God and Savior, we solemnly make this covenant with each other.

We will walk together in brotherly love, endeavoring to keep the unity of the Spirit in the bonds of peace. We will exercise a Christian care and watchfulness over each other and faithfully to admonish and help one another, as the need may be.

We will rejoice in each other's good, and with tenderness and sympathy bear one another's burdens.

We will not forsake the assembling of ourselves together, nor neglect to pray for ourselves and others.

Such as may be under our care we will endeavor to bring up in the nurture and admonition of the Lord, and we will seek to win our kindred and acquaintances to Christ and to a godly life.

As stewards of the Lord, we will aid in the support of a faithful evangelical ministry among us, and in efforts to preach the gospel to the whole human family.

We will sustain our pastor by our prayers and cooperation in the great work of the Gospel.

We will live circumspectly in the world, denying ungodliness and worldly lusts, and, according to our ability and opportunities, will do good to all men.

And we will endeavor, as long as we live, amidst evil report and good report, to glorify him who hath called us out of darkness into his marvelous light.

94 *THE APOSTLES' CREED*

I believe in God the Father Almighty, maker of heaven and earth; and in Jesus Christ his only Son our Lord; who was conceived by the

Holy Ghost; born of the Virgin Mary; suffered under Pontius Pilate; was crucified, dead, and buried; he descended into hell; the third day he rose again from the dead; he ascended into heaven; and sitteth on the right hand of God the Father Almighty; from thence he shall come to judge the quick and the dead. I believe in the Holy Ghost; the holy catholic church; the communion of saints; the forgiveness of sins; the resurrection of the body; and the life everlasting.

95 *THE KOREAN CREED*

We believe in the one God, maker and ruler of all things, Father of all men, the source of all goodness and beauty, all truth and love.

We believe in Jesus Christ, God manifest in the flesh, our teacher, example, and redeemer, the Savior of the world.

We believe in the Holy Spirit, God present with us for guidance, for comfort, and for strength.

We believe in the forgiveness of sins, in the life of love and prayer, and in grace equal to every need.

We believe in the Word of God contained in the Old and New Testaments as the sufficient rule both of faith and of practice.

We believe in the church as the fellowship for worship and for service of all who are united to the living Lord.

We believe in the kingdom of God as the divine rule in human society, and in the brotherhood of man under the fatherhood of God.

We believe in the final triumph of righteousness, and in the life everlasting.

96 *AN AFFIRMATION IN SCRIPTURAL LANGUAGE*

We believe that God is a spirit and they that worship him must worship him in spirit and in truth.

We believe that God hath made of one blood all nations of men to dwell on the face of the whole earth.

We believe that God is love, and every one that loveth is born of God and knoweth God.

We believe that Jesus is the Son of God, and as many as are led by the spirit of God, they are the sons of God.

We believe that the Lord Jesus is the way, the truth, and the life.

We believe that if we walk in the light, as he is in the light, we have fellowship one with another.

We believe that, if we confess our sins, God is faithful and just to forgive us our sins.

We believe that the world passeth away, and the lust thereof; but that he that doeth the will of God abideth forever.

97   *A CONFESSION OF FAITH IN SCRIPTURAL LANGUAGE*

God is a spirit, and they that worship him must worship him in spirit and in truth. God is light and in him is no darkness at all, neither shadow that is cast by turning. God is love and every one that loveth is begotten of God and knoweth God. Love never faileth, and there is no fear in love, but perfect love casteth out fear. So then we are debtors not to the flesh to live after the flesh, but we received the spirit of adoption whereby we cry Abba, Father. Being therefore always of good courage, we walk by faith, not by sight, and we make it our aim to be well pleasing unto him. For we know that, to them that love God, all things work together for good. And the peace of God, which passeth all understanding shall guard our hearts and our thoughts in Christ Jesus.

98   *AN AFFIRMATION OF FAITH*

We believe in God the Father, infinite in wisdom, goodness, and love; and in Jesus Christ, his Son, our Lord and Savior, who for us and our our salvation lived and died and rose again and liveth evermore; and in the Holy Spirit, who taketh of the things of Christ and revealeth them to us, renewing, comforting, and inspiring the souls of men.

We are united in striving to know the will of God as taught in the Holy Scriptures, and in our purpose to walk in the ways of the Lord, made known or to be made known to us.

We hold it to be the mission of the church of Christ to proclaim the gospel to all mankind, exalting the worship of the one true God, and laboring for the progress of knowledge, the promotion of justice, the reign of peace, and the realization of human brotherhood.

Depending, as did our fathers, upon the continued guidance of the Holy Spirit to lead us into all truth, we work and pray for the transformation of the world into the kingdom of God; and we look with faith for the triumph of righteousness and the life everlasting.

National Council of Congregational Churches

99   *A DECLARATION OF BELIEF*

I believe in God, the creator of heaven and of earth, Lord of all power
    and might;

I believe in Jesus Christ, in whom the grace and glory of God became
    incarnate;

I believe in the Holy Spirit, by whom the heavenly flame is brought to
    human souls;

I believe in the oneness of him who is made manifest in all things great
    and good.

    I acknowledge the law of God which is written in the majesty of
        suns and stars;

    I acknowledge the truth of God within which alone we can be free;

    I acknowledge the love of God by which alone we are redeemed;

    I acknowledge the fellowship of all saints.

        Who learned of Christ and lived for him,

        Who carried in their hearts the flame of consecration and of courage,

        Who dared and endured and triumphed even in defeat:

        The evangelists, the apostles, and the martyrs,

        The singers of the triumph of the soul,

        The lovers and the servants of mankind,

        Who gave their lives, and in the giving found all life fulfilled,

        Who in their gentleness were great.

Through them and unto God I lift my soul in thankfulness and in eternal
    praise.

Walter Russell Bowie

100   *A CHRISTIAN'S TESTIMONY*

I affirm my faith in the reality of the spiritual world, in the sacred
voice of duty, in the compelling power of truth and holiness, in prayer,
in the life eternal, in him who is the life of my life and the reality behind
all things visible. I rejoice to believe in God.

I reaffirm my discipleship and the dedication of my body and mind
to Jesus Christ, my Lord. I claim anew a share in his redemption and full
salvation. As he has been my Saviour to this day, so shall he be my
Saviour to the end. I merge all the power of my life in his redemptive
purpose and stand ready to bear the cross after him.

I affirm my faith in the Kingdom of God and my hope in its final triumph. I determine by faith to live day by day within the higher order and the divine peace of my true fatherland, and to carry its spirit and laws into all my dealings in the world that now is.

I make an act of love toward all my fellow men. I accept them as they are, with all their sins and failures, and declare my solidarity with them. If any have wronged or grieved me, I place my mind within the all-comprehending and all-loving mind of God, and here and now forgive. I desire to minister God's love to men and to offer no hindrance to the free flow of his love through me.

I affirm my faith in life. I call life good and not evil. I accept the limitations of my own life and believe it is possible for me to live a beautiful and Christlike life within the conditions set for me. Through the power of Christ which descends on me, which besets me behind and before, and which dwells in the innermost fastnesses of my spirit, I know that I can be more than conqueror.

Walter Rauschenbusch

101   *A PROFESSION OF FAITH*

I believe in the love of God through Jesus Christ.

I believe in the cross of Calvary as the ground plan of the universe.

I believe in the transcendental meaning and hope of life.

I believe that the true goods of life lie in the unseen, where Christ sitteth at the right hand of God.

I believe that the real values of life are the good, the true and the beautiful.

I believe in the salvability and immortality of every man, and in the infinite value of every living soul.

I believe in the practicability of the Kingdom of God, and in freedom to choose it and to work for it.

I believe in the sacramental quality of my day's work and that I may see and serve God in it.

I believe in a grace that can overcome my selfishness and pride, and that will enable me to overcome temptation, and upon which I need never call in vain.

I believe in love as the final law of life.

And in this faith, by the help of God, I mean to live this day and all my days.

Richard Roberts

102   *A PERSONAL AFFIRMATION*

I believe in God, who is for me spirit, love, the principle of all things.

I believe that God is in me, as I am in him.

I believe that the true welfare of man consists in fulfilling the will of God.

I believe that from the fulfilment of the will of God there can follow nothing but that which is good for me and for all men.

I believe that the will of God is that every man should love his fellow-men, and should act toward others as he desires that they should act toward him.

I believe that the reason of life is for each of us simply to grow in love.

I believe that this growth in love will contribute more than any other force to establish the kingdom of God on earth—to replace a social life in which division, falsehood, and violence are all-powerful, with a new order in which humanity, truth, and brotherhood will reign.

Leo Tolstoy

III. Resources for Communion Preaching and Communion Table Meditations

A. MEANINGS OF THE SUPPER

103   *RICHEST EXPERIENCE IN WORSHIP*

I love holy communion and have always loved it. To me it is the richest experience in worship that the church has to offer. I, too, can find God in nature or beside the sea or under the great arch of the sky, but nothing can take the place of being a part of that adoring company which gathers before his altar. I love its quietness, its singular and distinctive beauty. The greatest music and the greatest art are dedicated to it. I love the spiritual dignity and the reverence of the atmosphere which surrounds it. To the Christian who believes in Christ as the Son of God and who accepts the cross as the means of his personal salvation, holy communion is meaningful beyond all capacity of words to describe it. But no spiritually sensitive person, whatever his creed or lack of creed, can in sincerity kneel at the communion rail and partake of the symbols of the cross, and rise without feeling that in some mysterious way he has, for the moment, met with God.

Hughes Wagner

104   *DRAW NEAR WITH FAITH*

Here is a symbolic act that brings home, as no mere words can do, the great affirmations of the Christian faith. Here is a celebration that proclaims the possibility of forgiveness of sin, healing for sorrow, strength for the day, and peace within even amidst the most adverse conditions. Here for those who "draw near with faith" is the apprehension of a divine presence and power whereby the heart is cleansed, renewed and comforted. Here is the opportunity for self-commitment: "We offer and present unto thee, O Lord, our selves, our souls and bodies, to be a reasonable, holy and living sacrifice unto thee."

Ernest Fremont Tittle

105   *GATHERED AT A FAMILY HEARTH*

We have, in the celebration of the Lord's Supper, that subtle combination of simplicity and sublimity, of intimacy and ultimacy, of reverence and homeliness. We are priests worshipping in the heavenlies with our great High Priest whom we adore; we are kings gathered before the throne of the King of kings; but we are also children of our Father, gathered at the family hearth, intimately related to each other in him, in a relationship which breaks down every racial and blood barrier, every class barrier, and which is closer than any blood bond of national or family tie can be, because we are joined in the communion of his body and blood.

W. Robinson

106   *CHRIST COMES TO US*

It is the Lord's Supper which is the ordinance designed to maintain the church in the knowledge that, although she is composed of sinners, who stray from the true way of life, Christ does not forsake her but meets with his people and holds communion with them at the appointed place and, if they approach him in penitence and expectant faith, will always do so until he comes again in glory. . . . Christ does come to us, but he does not do so in the way in which he appeared in the days of his flesh nor as he will when he appears again in glory. He comes under the veils of the bread and wine. In themselves these elements have no power. They are signs, which have potency only as they point away from themselves to him whom they signify. The sacrament does express a continuity, but it is a continuity which is unintelligible except from within faith. We are at one with the disciples in the upper room and, by the judgment and promise of the Gospel, with Israel in Egypt on the night of the Passover. Yet we are at one with them as those who look with them for the passing away of this provisional arrangement for holding communion with their Lord and toward that day when we shall together drink of the fruit of the vine with our Lord in newness of life in glory. The sacramental meal assures us that our Lord has made provision for our not fainting with hunger in the present dispensation, but it never gives us more than sufficient for the next step of the journey, that we may ever look to him and for him "till he come" (1 Cor. 11:26).

Daniel Jenkins

107   *THE FOCUSING-POINT OF REVELATION*

The element of mystery is present in all real personal religion. There is no greater mystery than the communion of man with God, however mediated. If the word mystery is applied in a special sense to the eucharist, it is because the sacrament is a focusing-point, at which the revelation of the Eternal in time and space is apprehended as a reality belonging to the distant past, which is nevertheless present to faith. Here the communion of the soul with God, which in itself is beyond space and time, is inseparably connected with the revelation of God in history, in Palestine, during the reigns of Augustus and Tiberius, in the man Jesus of Nazareth, by his incarnation and his sacrifice of himself; and this communion may become actual, at all times and in all places, where an altar is raised and the solemn words are said: "The same night in which he was betrayed [he] took bread" (1 Cor. 11:23). This communion is spiritual, as all communion with God is spiritual; yet it draws the material within its sphere and operates through a material means, just as the revelation of the Eternal in time was mediated through flesh and blood, when in the mystery of the Incarnation he embraced his created world.

Yngve Brilioth

108   *THE BURNING HEART OF WORSHIP*

The climax of Christian corporate prayer is in the celebration of the sacrament. That was the burning heart of worship in the early church. It seems to have the fire of eternity. Neither theological strife, nor attempts to make it magic, nor seasons of ebbing zeal, nor the world's despisings have quenched its altar flame. The journeying generations are blessed by its light and warmth. How simple it is—a child may understand its tokens of bread and wine—yet how unfathomable its mystery! How lowly —bread and wine were on every poorest table—yet how awe-filled and alone! How comradely—it was the Sabbath meal in the early church— yet how sharp in individual challenge and redemption! How rich in symbolism—as wheat is sown in darkness, lives again to be cut by the reaper, is ground between millstones, and thus becomes man's nourishment, so is the sacrificial love of Christ; as grapes are trodden in the winepress, so is his bruised body and outpoured blood—how rich in symbolism, yet how intangibly real! How stored with history—it has been the benediction of vast cathedral and lonely bedside, the solace of Covenanter and priest—yet how instant in a Presence!

George A. Buttrick

109   *THE CENTRAL ACT OF WORSHIP*

From the upper room there stretches an unbroken chain of light— like a chain of fires burning in the darkness—down the centuries to our own day. For the eucharist is the central act of Christian worship.

Wherever the church takes root, there its life is quickened, nourished, and manifested in the celebration of the sacrament. Just as the first thing we do in a new house is to light a fire, and the fire warms and hallows the new house, so wherever men have gone in their wanderings, the sacrament has gone with them. For Christ is our home throughout the journey of life: "He that is near me is near the Fire."

The eucharist is central: because it gathers up, expresses, and makes effective the whole meaning of the spiritual life. It proclaims the Christian Gospel: in it God comes to us with his forgiveness and his strength. One by one, and as members of the body of Christ, we respond to him with gratitude and awe.

The meaning of the eucharist is inexhaustible; it transcends all our efforts to explain or interpret it. We never come to the end of it. Long experience only deepens our wonder and our awe. In every age, in every part of the Church Universal, both in corporate worship and in the experience of the individual, glimpses are sometimes granted of the glory which lies behind the sacrament: one part· of the church will see one aspect, and another will see something else, but the truth, the glory and the depth of the eucharist are beyond us all.

Olive Wyon

110   *MADE TRULY GOD'S PEOPLE*

Why should this be the moment in all their existence when the people of God are most *truly* the people of God.

1. Pre-eminently, the service is *an enactment of the gospel,* that God in Christ has come to us and by his sacrificial death redeemed our lives. The Bible describes this, sermons talk about it, but the sacrament *dramatizes* it. Calvin, following Augustine, called it "the Word made visible."

2. *By partaking of the elements, we indicate that we wish Christ to dwell in our hearts by faith.* At other times we may talk about our faith; here we act it out. As we take the bread and wine into our physical bodies, we are indicating by that action our wish that Christ enter into us. And the sacrament itself is God's promise that he does.

3. Not only are we joined with him, but *we are also united in a new way with our fellow believers.* Here is when *koinonia,* or fellowship, is most real. We are not just individuals before God, but we are a community united together before God. . . . Here is where "the communion of saints" is most real. As the eucharistic prayer reminds us, we are "in the com-

munion of all the faithful in heaven and on earth." We are not just "present company" praising God; we are joining in the perpetual chorus of praise that is offered to God by "all the company of heaven." Since God is "the King of all creation," his children in all of creation can be one at this particular moment.

4. The service underlies *the significance of our everyday life*. We bring bread and wine (God's gifts in the first place), the symbols of our earthly toil, and get back Christ. God uses common things as channels of his revelation. The act of eating can make God more real than a stained-glass window. The act of drinking can make God more real than a fifty-voice robed choir. There is nothing too ordinary to be used by him. All of life is sacred and holy.

Robert McAfee Brown

111   *ELEMENTS OF WORSHIP*

The framework of a modern liturgy of the Lord's Supper ought . . . to consist of six steps, about as follows:

1. *Confession and forgiveness*. Here, minister and people would strive to purge their minds of all that might hinder a complete spiritual identification with the purpose of the sacramental hour. If a declaration of forgiveness or "absolution" is included, it would of course be in the first person plural—"we" and "us," not "I" and "you."

2. *Instruction*. The second step would consist of reading from the Scriptures, or a sermon, or both.

3. *Devotional preparation for communion*. Within this third stage would be found devotional materials which would generally include, as invariable elements, the Comfortable Words, the *Sursum Corda,* and the *Sanctus*.

4. *The blessing of the bread and the cup*. At this point, the bread would be blessed and broken by the minister, and the cup "taken," or held in the minister's hands before the congregation, accompanied by the repetition of Jesus' words of institution.

5. *Communion*. Here the bread and contents of the cup are distributed to the congregation, by whatever method is customary in the church.

6. *Thanksgiving and praise*. Not by any means the least important phase of such a liturgy would be post-communion prayers in the spirit of thanksgiving and praise to God for his gifts symbolized in the sacrament.

Elmer S. Freeman

112   *THE GREAT THANKSGIVING*

Even in times of persecution, when to meet for the Lord's memorial was to disobey the law and run the risk of torture and death, when at every meeting new names were added to the list of martyrs to be remembered before the Lord, the celebration was marked by the greatest joy and gladness. It was held as a feast of life, and not of death. The communicants bore themselves as those who knew that theirs was the victory that overcometh the world, and that with them was the power that could cast down the strongholds of cruelty and wickedness. Each communion was a repetition to them of the joy of Easter. They were like men who had been brought from darkness and terror into light and peace, and who for the spirit of heaviness had received the garment of praise. Therefore the burden of all their worship was "Thanks be to God," and the holy communion was to them the eucharist, the great thanksgiving.

J. T. Levens

113   *ASPECTS OF THE FEAST*

What Christ does for us here is unsearchably rich in meaning. Plainly enough, this central fact of the church's life has many aspects, yet three aspects have been determinative from the beginning. There is, first, the historical or memorial aspect; we remember here what was said and done in time by Jesus; this feast is a memorial feast, commemorating the mightiest of God's mighty acts of grace in the cross and the resurrection. There is, second, the timeless or eternal aspect. Here we are lifted out of time and have communion with the very life of God. The feast mediates God's presence and his very self to us: here our fellowship with God and in God has all the actuality and wholeness of life. Thirdly, when by an act of faith we partake together of bread and wine in this sacrament, these two aspects become one. At this table there is a unique fusion or synthesis of what is historical and what is beyond history; of what is in time and is remembered, and what is timeless and is experienced.

J. S. Whale

114   *PERSPECTIVES OF THE SUPPER*

For those who had been present at the Last Supper, the breaking of bread had a peculiar significance and pathos which it cannot have for us.

On the other hand, there is a wealth of meaning in the rite for us which was beyond their grasp, for we know, as they could not, the long history of the church of Christ throughout the centuries. The story of the church does not add to the Word of God, but it enriches, explains and illuminates the Scriptures. Implicit in the New Testament are several moments which properly find their place in the administration of the rite. There is first the backward look to the Last Supper and to Calvary—"this do . . . in remembrance of me" (1 Cor. 11:25); there is, second, the forward look to the bridal supper of the Lamb in the perfected Kingdom—"till I come" (Rev. 2:25); there is, third, the feeding upon Christ by faith—"take, eat; this is my body" (Matt. 26:26); there is, fourth, the church as the Body of Christ—"as my Father hath sent me, even so send I you" (John 20:21); fifth, the rite is eucharist, the church's thanksgiving in the confession of the Redeemer's name, *sacrificium laudis;* it is *sacrificium propitiatorium* only as it may mystically be regarded as an extension of the Passion into time. Above and before all there is the real presence of the Lord himself as surely as on that last betrayal night, sealing his promise to believers and giving himself unto his own.

Nathaniel Micklem

115   From *JOHN WESLEY'S JOURNAL (June 28, 1740)*

I showed at large: 1. That the Lord's Supper was ordained by God to be a means of conveying to men either preventing, or justifying, or sanctifying grace, according to their several necessities. 2. That the persons for whom it was ordained are all those who know and feel that they want the grace of God, either to restrain them from sin, or to show their sins forgiven, or to renew their souls in the image of God. 3. That inasmuch as we come to his table, not to give him anything, but to receive whatsoever he sees best for us, there is no previous preparation indispensably necessary, but a desire to receive whatsoever he pleases to give. And 4. That no fitness is required at the time of communicating, but a sense of our own state, of our utter sinfulness and helplessness; every one who knows he is fit for hell being just fit to come to Christ in this as well as all other ways of his appointment.

116   *THE HOLY COMMUNION*

A pledge of communion (Acts 2:42)
A memorial of the dispensation (Eph. 3:2)

A showing forth of his death (1 Cor. 11:26)
A communion of body and blood (Luke 22:19)
A sharing in the Spirit (1 Cor. 12:13)
Remission of sins (Matt. 26:28)
A riddance of things contrary (1 Cor. 5:7)
Rest of conscience (Matt. 11:29)
Blotting out of debts (Col. 2:14)
Cleansing of stains (Heb. 9:14)
Healing of the soul's sicknesses (1 Pet. 2:24)
Renewing of the covenant (Ps. 2:5)
Food of spiritual life (John 6:27)
Increase of strengthening grace (Heb. 13:9)
And of winning consolation (Luke 2:25)
Compunction of penitence (2 Cor. 7:9)
Illumination of mind (Luke 24:31)
Exercise of humility (1 Pet. 5:5)
Seal of faith (2 Cor. 1:22)
Fulness of wisdom (Rom. 11:33)
Bond of love (John 13:35)
Call for a collection (1 Cor. 16:1)
A means of endurance (1 Pet. 4:1)
Liveliness of thanksgiving (Ps. 116:12)
Confidence of prayer (Ps. 116:13)
Mutual indwelling (John 6:56)
Pledge of the resurrection (John 6:34)
Acceptable defence in judgment (Luke 14:18)
Covenant of the inheritance (Luke 22:20)
Figure of perfection (John 17:23)

Lancelot Andrewes

117   *THE VARIED SIGNIFICANCE IN THE RITE*

None of his people can think of their Lord's death without thanksgiving for the redemption which he wrought, and a eucharistic element must therefore be present. Nor can it be supposed that this is in any way exceptionable. Moreover, the sacrament is a present experience. "Take, eat" and "Drink ye" are found to refer not merely to the symbols, but to him whom they represent, who may be received into our hearts to order our lives. The element of communion is therefore to be found here —communion with Christ and communion with the church, which, no less than the bread, though in a different way, is the Body of Christ. It is no accident that the Fourth Gospel gives the discourse on the True Vine in its account of the Last Supper in the upper room, where Jesus calls for a oneness with himself as intimate as the union of the branch and the tree. Moreover, since this is no individual feast, its social significance for the fellowship of the church of Christ, which must draw all its life from him and which must therefore know a profound unity of spirit when it is truly in him, cannot be overlooked or forgotten. Further, this rite is a sacrament, not merely in the sense of something sacred and ministering grace to the believer, but in the sense that the word *sacramentum* acquired in Latin, *viz.*, a vow of loyalty. "This is my blood of the *covenant*" (Mark 14:24), or "This cup is the new *covenant* in my blood" (Luke 22:20), reminds us that here as ever we deal with something that is two-sided. We receive enrichment of the covenant that we may renew the covenant by bringing afresh the spirit of our consecration.

H. H. Rowley

118   *WHAT THE SUPPER MEANS*

In God's providence we are invited to come together of set purpose, and to share in a sacred rite which means all these things to us: that God knows us, and that his knowledge of us has not abated his loving purpose towards us; that he is prepared to forgive us our sins, and to take us anew into his love; that it will not be possible for us to draw near to him and to touch the hem of Christ's garment without coming away the better equipped for life; and that face to face with this passing show of a world, we are in contact here and now with One who is the same yesterday, today, and forever.

John A. Hutton

119   *INCORPORATE INTO CHRIST THE VINE*

It is difficult to determine what meaning the early Christians attached to the eucharist. Most of them, even the ministers, were very simple people, and experienced much more than they could express or define. Some theologians have tried to find in such fragments of early eucharistic teaching as we possess the germ of the fully developed doctrine of the later church; others have denied that any such indications are to be found. It is almost certain that, in early days, the eschatological element was strongly marked; the eucharist was the earthly anticipation of the messianic banquet, of the final triumph of Christ. It is probable that the minds of the early Christians were strongly realist. In this ordinance, they felt themselves incorporate into Christ the vine, the head of the body. When to be in Christ was literally a matter of life and death, there was little time for speculation. It is unlikely that we shall find in their testimony answers to questions which had not yet been asked.

Stephen Neill

120   THE NEED OF ENLARGED HEARTS

Except ye eat the flesh of the Son of man, and drink his blood, ye have no life in you. JOHN 6:53

This is the true bread which cometh down from heaven, of which if a man eat he will hunger no more. Now we come with our little dwarfing expositions, and take all the sap, the juice, the wine out of this holy growth. We will ask little questions about transubstantiation, and we will set up little enigmas and miserable riddles which are unworthy of the Christian imagination, and our religious liberties and privileges. This is not a question of transubstantiation: the bread does not pass into any other body or substance: the wine is wine at the last as at the first, and no magic can change its nature. And yet as in the letter I feel the spirit, so in these elements of bread and wine my heart feels that it is feasting upon the living Lord. Do not ask for this gospel to be reduced to words: I ask you to enlarge your words to receive this gospel.

Joseph Parker

121   REALITY IN RELIGION

Our Savior gave the world the blessed sacrament to keep religion a reality. Lest thoughts of God should drift into hazy sentimentalism, he left the living memorial of his being, his vital personality, and his effectual death. The holy communion is an extension of the stable at Bethlehem, the shop at Nazareth, the miracles of the seashore, the teachings of the hillside, the agony of the cross, and the radiance of resurrection. It was to substitute all this and precisely this in our distracted souls that Jesus bequeathed this definite activity to us, his disciples. The soul craves something to do, to be, to follow, to measure by, to add to its little self. It was to define the self as needy and incomplete yet beloved of God, and to define God as a loving and seeking fatherhood, that this distillation of the career of Christ was instituted. The holy communion is definite, something to try to be worthy of, something to add to our selves, something to feed upon.

S. S. Drury

122 *CHRISTIANITY VALIDATED*

The holy communion . . . is one of the strongest proofs of the truth of Christianity. Here is a rite whose observance is practically universal among all Christians today. The same universality of observance existed in the ages before our own, for the rite has come down to us in unbroken sequence from the past. Step by step we can trace back this memorial of Christ through the centuries, finding no break in the observance amid the fall of old empires and the rise of new nations, or the shifting boundaries of peoples and tongues. We find it celebrated in Gothic cathedrals and Roman basilicas, in the hidden passages of the catacombs and in caves of the African desert, in obscure streets of Alexandria, Corinth, and Antioch, until we reach the upper room in Jerusalem where the first memorial was made. The rite is a witness whose testimony cannot be gainsaid, a sure proof of the historic reality of the facts that are commemorated. It is a creed in act, chronicling and representing the essential truths of the Christian faith.

J. T. Levens

123 *THE FLYING BUTTRESSES OF THE CHURCH*

Even most good Christians do not know what to make of the sacraments: baptism and the Lord's Supper. They are venerable customs which have always been performed by the church, in which one takes part out of respect, or because they are here and are observed—or perhaps simply out of habit, or "because it makes things better." In the cities, the neglect of the Lord's Supper is quite general. Often no more than a fourth of the many who throng the church on high festivals remain for the Lord's Supper. Are the sacraments dying branches on the tree of the church—like so much that once was customary, but is now sacrificed to the times?

The Lord surely knew what he was doing when, on that last night, he said to his disciples, "This do in remembrance of me" (Luke 22:10). Without the sacraments the church would long ago have disappeared, and with the passing of the church would have gone also Christian faith and the Bible. The sacraments are the divinely given flying buttresses which save the church from collapse. In how many of the churches of today do we not find the sacraments almost the sole biblical footing—the only biblical element that has been able to withstand the caprices of the gifted minister who lives by his own wisdom rather than from the Scriptures. Even the most audacious minister has not dared to lay hands on the sacraments. And they are what they are! One may so interpret the words of Scripture that the words speak the opposite of their intent; but the sacraments, thank God, speak a language independent of the language of the pastor. They are a part of the message of the church least affected by theological or other tendencies; and that is their especial blessing.

Emil Brunner

B. LIGHT FROM THE UPPER ROOM

124   *TOUCHED WITH A SPLENDOR OF GLORY*

There was once a garret up under the roof—a poor, bare place enough. There was a table in it, and there were some benches, and a water-pot; a towel and a basin in behind the door—but not much else—a bare, unhomelike room. But the Lord Christ entered into it. And, from that moment, it became the holiest of all, where souls innumerable ever since have met the Lord God, in his glory, face to face. And, if you give him entrance to that very ordinary heart of yours, it, too, he will transform and sanctify and touch with a splendor of glory.

Arthur John Gossip

125   *THE MASTER'S DESIRE*

"With desire I have desired to eat this passover with you before I suffer" (Luke 22:15). He remembers the anointing at Bethany. He remembers what strength it brought him. He remembers how the communion of one human heart had braced him for his burial. Would not the effect be repeated by the communion of *twelve* human hearts representative of twelve times twelve thousand? The desire of Jesus was a desire for personal stimulus. I do not think it was a wish to say farewell. I do not think he ever looked upon the Last Supper as a farewell. The consciousness on his part was *not* that of impending separation. He did not feel that he was bidding his disciples good-bye. He wished to meet them for a very different purpose. He wished, before entering that Gethsemane which death still held for him, to gaze on the few gems which he had already won for his Father.

George Matheson

126   *THE GREATEST EVENING IN HIS LIFE*

The Thursday evening arrived, when in every house in Jerusalem the Passover was eaten. Jesus also with the twelve sat down to eat it. He knew that it was his last night on earth, and that this was his farewell meeting with his own. Happily there has been preserved to us a full account of it, with which every Christian mind is familiar. It was the greatest evening in his life. His soul overflowed in indescribable tenderness and grandeur. Some shadows indeed fell across his spirit in the earlier hours of the evening. But they soon passed; and throughout the scenes of the washing of the disciples' feet, the eating of the Passover, the institution of the Lord's Supper, the farewell address, and the great high-priestly prayer, the whole glory of his character shone out. He completely resigned himself to the genial impulses of friendship, his love of his own flowing forth without limit; and, as if he had forgotten all their imperfections, he rejoiced in the anticipation of their future successes and the triumph of his cause. Not a shadow intercepted his view of the face of his Father or dimmed the satisfaction with which he looked on his own work just about to be completed. It was as if the passion were already past, and the glory of his exaltation were already breaking around him.

James Stalker

127   COMRADES IN THE NEW COMMUNITY

The food was placed on the table—the lamb and the unleavened loaves to recall how the Hebrews had on the night of the flight from Egypt eaten the lamb and the bread that had been so hurriedly made ready; the salad of bitter herbs—coriander and endive, lettuce and horehound, thistle leaves and succory—to recall the harsh savour of Egyptian slavery; the thin brick of crushed fruit and nuts—bringing to mind the work of brickmaking under the lash. . . .

One handed a cup to him. The Passover cup all through the centuries has stood for the covenant that the Eternal made with Abraham to be the God of his children and his children's children for ever. Jesus gave thanks to God for it, saying in the ritual words of the Passover Supper, "Blessed be he who created the fruit of the vine." . . . . So they went through the regular order of the Passover, eating the lamb, dipping the bitter herbs in the crushed fruits, and singing to God's praise.

Jesus then took up in his hands one of the flat, circular loaves and, giving thanks to God for the bread, he broke it in pieces with his fingers, as is the custom always at the Passover [and] to each of his men he handed a morsel. . . . The eating of the Passover food was now over. Then Jesus took the cup of red wine mingled with water, and made it the token, no longer of the old covenant between God and Abraham, but of a new covenant between Jesus and a new people—those who were to go as his disciples in the Kingdom of God, and so, as children of one Father, they were, of whatever race or nation, all comrades in the new community—brothers in a new family. . . .

It was a moment of deep sadness and of immortal promise. It was the very symbol of his dying, but it was the beginning of a new life for the whole world. He began at that hour a brotherhood of all peoples in all ages, whose oneness is that they are his body.

Basil Mathews

128   *THEY HAD NOT QUIT*

One of the most moving scenes in the Gospels, so it seems to me, is that moment in the upper room when, as Luke tells us, Jesus looked round on his disciples and said: "It is you who have stood by me through my trials" (Luke 22:28, Moffatt). That was rather fine of him. Those first disciples had not done so well. They had continually failed to understand him and had let him down. Peter was there, soon to deny him thrice. Even at the table, Luke tells us, a contention rose among them as to who was the greatest. They were not much to be grateful for.

To be sure, this much can be said for them—they had not altogether quit. The brief years of Jesus' ministry had been difficult, opposition mounting, foes dangerously massed against him, many and powerful, and yet despite weakness and failure those few men in the upper room were still at his side. At least they had not quit, and for that much Jesus was grateful: "You who have stood by me."

Harry Emerson Fosdick

129   *THEY STUCK TO THE POINT*

Let us go into the upper room and consider the company gathered there. Who are these people? They are very ordinary folk, not a superman among them, no one of outstanding intellect, no likely statesman. Even the eleven apostles, the inner circle, were so far men of no special distinction. Indeed, their story in the gospels shows them to have been rather dull, slow in the uptake and laying a heavy tax upon the singular patience of Jesus. Evidently Jesus did not choose them for their cleverness, their public ability; yet Jesus did choose them, and he must have had good reasons for choosing them. We are not told what these reasons were; but we may at least divine one of the reasons. Jesus had said to them, "Ye are they which have continued with me in my [trials]"

(Luke 22:28). They had staying power and had proved it. They might be stupid, but they had been faithful. Jesus knew that once they had seen the point, they would stick to it, and the story St. Luke has to tell is in great part the story of how these men stuck to the point. Jesus chose them for their moral qualities. . . . He was not looking for brilliancy but for steadfastness, for men for spade work, not men for fireworks.

Richard Roberts

130   *THE DISCIPLES PUT ON GUARD*

I remember one afternoon watching the Bremen steam out of the placid harbor at Cherbourg into the black maw of a hurricane, white and majestic in one last gleam of sunlight before the tumult closed in and blotted her out of sight. That's what was happening to the men who sat listening to Jesus in the quiet of that last evening around the table. They were destined shortly, all of them, to face the wind and the dark. Whatever problem is posed for the human mind and heart by the existence of evil in a world of God, they were headed for it. . . . Tomorrow on the hill there would be a cross, and life would start going bitterly wrong, as at a signal. It would seem like a ghastly world for such good people, with nothing much but contempt and death waiting around every corner, and God just standing by doing nothing. . . . Many a time they would look up amazed and hurt and bewildered. He only hoped they wouldn't be unsteadied by it. Perhaps if they remembered then how he had told them of it before, that would help. And it did. I am sure of it. Life might go bitterly wrong, but it wasn't bitterly insane and senseless. He had understood it. Jesus had at least put them on their guard against the savage ills of living!

Paul Scherer

131   *SPIRITUALLY ADEQUATE*

You might have told that band of disciples, behind closed doors for fear, that since Jesus had risen from the dead there was nothing to be afraid of. But that would not have taken them out from behind those closed doors. There was only one way to get them out and that was to raise the tone of the inner life so that they were inwardly a match for outer circumstances. Pentecost gave them that inner adequacy. Inner life became adequate for outer life. Henceforth nothing could stop them.

Fears fell away as irrelevancies. Out of that upper room which had been the place of fears they burst with the glad good news. They smiled at poverty, rejoiced under stripes, were elated at their humiliations, sang in midnight prisons, courted death and shared with every man, everywhere, their own abundant life. God had matched them against that need and they were spiritually adequate.

E. Stanley Jones

132   *THE RELEVANCE OF THE UPPER ROOM*

And he said, Go into the city to such a man, and say unto him, The Master saith, My time is at hand; I will keep the passover at thy house with my disciples. And the disciples did as Jesus had appointed them; and they made ready the passover. Now when the even was come, he sat down with the twelve.   MATTHEW 26:18-20

To that upper room of many memories our thoughts return at every sacrament season. We see the Master and his friends reclining at the holy table. We sense the quiet intimacy of that mystic fellowship. We hear the rise and fall of the dear voice as it speaks its never-to-be-forgotten words of parting and solace. We finger lovingly the precious pages of St. John, burdened with the prayers and promises of that immortal hour. We think of the generations of men and women who have nourished their devotional life and revived their thirsty souls at those unfailing springs. . . . To that upper room of long ago and far away, that quiet sanctuary amid the clash and clamour of the world, the heart of Christendom continually returns. Here, if anywhere, is holy ground. . . . Now comes the question, urgent, challenging: Is this thing we are doing here relevant? Has it any sense in a world like [ours]? Is it not frightfully incongruous and inapposite?

James S. Stewart

133   *LIFE'S UPPER ROOMS*

The activities and rewards of the time are so engrossing that many high-minded and pure-hearted people find no time for meditation and communion in the upper room. Many of them are so bent on helping their fellows that they forget whence cometh their help; they are so eager to share the sorrows of their fellows that they forget him who bore the cross up the steep way to Calvary; they are so drained by the duties they take up that they lose the inspiration which makes duty the channel through which love pours itself out; they listen with such passionate attention to the cries for help that come from the world around them that they no longer hear the still, small voice of the Father of all men. In the house of the generous and self-sacrificing, as in the houses of the selfish and hard-hearted, there is no upper room.

And yet no man can live without God! It is true, he comes in a thousand forms and speaks many languages; but it is also true that men must make ready the room in which they can meet him face to face. Where there is no upper room, the house, however nobly appointed and dedicated, may remain a place of courage and arduous endeavor, but it ceases to be a place of contagious hope, of that vision which enables men to look at the sorrows of the arid lives without losing heart in the infinite love. For those who give themselves to works of mercy and stand ready to help in the highways, no less than for those who feed their bodies and starve their souls, the upper room is not only a place of refuge, it is a necessity of the higher nature; and the more exacting the work becomes, and the greater its interest and reward, the more pressing is the need of the upper room where the tumult of the world dies into silence and the ambitions of the world shrink into the rewards of a passing hour, and man talks with his God.

Hamilton Wright Mabie

C. CHRIST, THE TABLE'S HOST

134   AT ONE WITH US

The sacraments declare Christ's intention to unite us to himself, to have fellowship with his own, to be at one with us. . . . He is present as the holy One before whom we are constrained to acknowledge our own unworthiness. He is present as the gracious One who endured the cross for our redemption. He is present as the Victor over sin and death, the living Lord of an eternal kingdom. In his presence, we are in the presence of the Eternal. Awe, reverence, wonder, adoring love possess us. Is it really surprising that the presence of the Lord and the fellowship he enters into with those who respond to him with faith cannot be contained in conceptual statement or be exhausted in verbal expression?

Elmer J. F. Arndt

135   WILL CHRIST COME TO THE FEAST?

What think ye, that he will not come to the feast?   JOHN 11:56

We meet on this appointed day not only to have fellowship with each other, but also to have fellowship with Jesus Christ. We call this season our communion season, not as though all life may not be communion, but because now we long, with undivided hearts, after communion with our Lord and Savior. Others may be absent from the table, and yet the table may be rich in blessing. . . . But if Christ be absent, our meeting is in vain. Our sacrament is but a wasted hour. Our common handling of the bread and wine can leave us no better than it found us. What think ye, then, will he come to the feast today?

That is the most vital of all questions. Will you allow me to tell you why I think Christ will not disappoint us at this hour? I think that he will come because the feast is his . . . because I know he loves to come . . . because he has so often come before . . . because we are a company of sinners.

George H. Morrison

136   CHRIST AT HIS TABLE

I believe that if our eyes were open to the unseen, we should indeed behold our Lord present at our communions. There and then, assuredly, if anywhere and at any time, he remembers his promise, "Where two or three are gathered together in my name, there am I in the midst of them" (Matt. 18:20). Such special presence, the promised congregational presence, is perfectly mysterious in mode but absolutely true in fact; no creation of our imagination or emotion but an object of our faith. I believe that our Lord so present, not *on* the holy table, but *at* it, would be seen himself in our presence to bless the bread and wine for a holy use, and to distribute them to his disciples. . . . I believe that we should worship him, thus present in the midst of us in his living grace, with unspeakable reverence, thanksgiving, joy and love. We should receive the bread and wine with a profound sense of their sacredness as given by him in physical assurance of our part, as believers in him and so as members of him, in all the benefits of his passion.

Handley C. G. Moule

137   *THE MARKS OF CHRIST'S PRESENCE*

The presence of Christ which we have in the Supper may be regarded as marked by these features. It is, first of all, *spiritual,* having nothing about it that is external or sensuous, fanciful or magical. It is also *vital,* not only because it touches the inner life of those that use it, but also because, carrying with it all the grace and strength of Christ's body and blood, it really nourishes their whole spiritual nature. In this respect it might also be called *direct,* because the Supper is not an instrument only by which Christ from afar influences the soul, but a channel whereby he himself comes into closest contact with the soul and puts forth on it, by the Spirit, his healing power. This presence is *active* too, because Jesus, in the Supper influences and stimulates the active energies of his disciples, not using their hearts as a silent shrine, but rather as a platform for the manifestation of his might. And it is also *perpetual,* because though the occasion of communion may pass away, and the measure of the communication change, the presence of Christ, as the Lord of the whole life, is to a regenerate soul a gift that shall never be alienated.

J. P. Lilley

138   *OUR SOUL'S FOOD*

In regarding Christ as the Bread of Life, we are not to restrict ourselves to the one benefit mentioned by him in instituting the feast, the remission of sins, but to have in view all his benefits tending to our spirtual nourishment and growth in grace. Christ is the Bread of Life in all his offices. As a prophet, he supplies the bread of divine truth to feed our minds; as a priest, he furnishes the bread of righteousness to satisfy our troubled consciences; as a king, he presents himself to us as an object of devotion, that shall fill our hearts, and whom we may worship without fear of idolatry.

As often as the Lord's Supper is celebrated we are invited to contemplate Christ as the food of our souls in this comprehensive sense. As often as we eat the bread and drink the cup we declare that Christ has been, and is now, our soul's food in all these ways. And as often as we use this Supper with sincerity we are helped to appropriate Christ as our spiritual food more and more abundantly.

Alexander Balmain Bruce

139   *A NEW EXPERIENCE OF BROTHERHOOD*

In what way is Christ present? He is at the head of the feast. To the devout worshipper in the holy communion the ministrant fades; all that is visible melts into invisible glory. It is Christ who is again breaking the bread and pouring the wine, and through these sacramental elements is bestowing upon his last disciples the same inner essence of his life and character which he gave to his first disciples in the Jerusalem upper room. He is giving the quality of himself which we may call the will to be broken, to be poured out, that God's utter love may be known in the lives of men. It is not outward form, it is not dramatic action, it is not parable; it is contact, presence, the personal communication of divine life to human life. They will remember that the church is called the body of Christ; and through the holy communion they will enter into a new experience of brotherhood. They will count that reception of the sacrament most sacred when they have knelt with all sorts and conditions of men, and have felt the glow of a relationship which includes all humanity, because for all humanity Christ broke his body, that he might be found in his new body, the church.

Charles L. Slattery

140   *THE STRENGTHENING FRIENDSHIP*

The realization of any friendship means the realization of power. If two people become real friends, then, in the respects in which one is strong and the other admires that strength, that strength, through communion, will pass to the weaker. The effort of the weaker to be strong is not the most powerful agency at work. The most effective agency is the friendship itself. The two friends will tend to become like one another, and both be stronger than before. This is true whether it be the strength of evil or of good. One nature does feed on another, the weaker on the stronger, so that where one Friend is Perfect Strength we can think of all his weaker brethren feeding on him; a fact which we symbolize in the holy communion, for in communion with Jesus our very souls feed on his nature as our bodies feed on bread. He is the "bread of God . . . which cometh down from heaven, and giveth life unto the world" (John 6:33).

Leslie D. Weatherhead

141   THE LIVING PRESENCE

A grandmother in New England recently asked, "Why do not young people read Emerson now as they did in my youth?" Emerson's advice is as sound as ever, but in our fast-moving age we feel that we have to turn around and look back at Emerson. He seems a voice out of the past and we are too hurried to stop and translate his wise words from their quiet setting into the tumult of our time. Not so with Christ. We can feel him beside us in Cleveland or Calcutta. He is our contemporary guide.

Or consider Lincoln. Often in these days when we are longing for national leadership, we hear men say, "If only Lincoln were alive." But even Lincoln seems dated by a day that is gone. We do not feel him beside us. We do not hold communion services with Lincoln. Yet that is just what we do with Christ. His is the living presence we sense at the communion altar.

Ralph W. Sockman

142   HE GIVES HIMSELF

Just as the sun shines most brightly at midday, so the love of the Son of God shines most gloriously in this wonderful Supper. Here he has opened his divine heart wide to us, like a rose in full bloom. He does not give me his garment or his picture, nor silver nor gold . . . but himself. When I approach him I see him, in spirit, wounded for our sakes, and I hear him say: "Come unto me, all of you." When I leave the table my soul saith: "My Friend is mine and I am his."

Christian Scriver

D. OF BREAD AND WINE

143   *PARTAKERS OF HIS LIFE*

The deepest purpose of the sacrament is not only to help us to think about [Christ], and to be grateful to him, but also to bring us into vital, spiritual fellowship with him, so that we shall have his mind in us, and be partakers of his nature; so that his life shall be reproduced in our lives, and we shall in some measure learn to see the world with his eyes, to think as he thought, and to feel as he felt, and to act as he acted. This is the real significance of the symbolism of the Supper. The bread and wine represent the body and the blood of Christ; his body is his personality, and the blood is the vital element of it, which is love. Now just as the bread and the wine of which we partake are taken up by the organs of digestion and assimilation, and become part of ourselves, bone of our bone and flesh of our flesh, so by our thought and our love the spiritual elements of Christ's personality, his thought and his love, become part of us; we become partakers of his life, of his nature. There is nothing miraculous about this; it is precisely the same thing that happens to us when we are brought into living sympathy with any strong, wise, loving human spirit. Something of his strength and wisdom and love passes into our spirits, and becomes part of ourselves. And precisely thus in our communion with the spiritual Christ do we become partakers of his life.

Washington Gladden

144   *AGENTS THAT SUSTAIN LIFE*

If we allow the mind to dwell for a while on the processes by which both bread and wine become agents to sustain life, we begin to perceive how eloquent and how deep their symbolism is. For, once, the bread was the seed, which had to lie buried in the ground, before it became first the blade, then the ear, then the full corn in the ear. When it reached its golden maturity, the sickle was laid to its stalk, and after it had been harvested and garnered, it was first ground into meal and then baked on the fire, before it was ready to change its life into new life in the bodies of men. A deeper parallel to the processes by which spiritual nourishment is communicated can hardly be conceived, except it be in the case of the wine, which is also set on the table. For, once, that wine was the life-blood of some living clusters that hung on a vine. Lowly, on the rocky hillsides, the vine-trees grow, pruned continually with sharp knives that they may bring forth more fruit. Even their little time of beauty is denied them, for as soon as the grapes come to their purple fulness, they are plucked and flung into the wine-press, where, literally, they are trodden under the foot of man; thus becoming fit to fill the cup, and to be used to slake man's thirst. After the same manner also is conveyed to man's spirit the "wine of the soul in mercy shed." The parallelism is arresting and complete.

J. R. P. Sclater

145   EVERY MAN A FACTOR

There is great significance in the fact that the raw material of the eucharist is bread and wine, for these elements are provided by the joint co-operation of the material realm and man. The bringing of the bread and wine to the altar involves a combination of human activities whose range and complexity elude the grasp of the human imagination. There is the labor of the men who have ploughed the wheatfield and sown and reaped and milled the grain, of those who have planted and harvested the vine, of those who have baked the bread and fermented the grape juice, and of all the vast mass of human beings who have directly or indirectly, and knowingly or unknowingly, been concerned with the making of the eucharistic elements and their conveyance to the place where the sacrament is to be celebrated. . . . It is literally impossible to exclude anyone from *some* share, remote or proximate, in this activity, and the elements as they are offered on the altar focus into themselves this unimaginably complex human co-operation, with all the sin, as well as all the virtue, that is implicated in it.

E. L. Mascall

146   THE PARABLES OF BREAD AND WINE

The Lord's Supper . . . was, in the first place, essentially a thing of symbols. It was a parable, as [Karl von] Weizsäcker has rightly said; "the last parable that we possess from the mouth of Jesus," as Jülicher calls it. [He] reminds us of our Lord's frequent habit of speaking twin-parables, or pairs of parables, in which the second member of the pair repeats the truth that has been already illustrated in the first, while setting it in fresh lights and adding new suggestions. Thus we have such doublets as the tares and the drag-net, the mustard seed and the leaven, the hidden treasure and the pearl of great price, the lost sheep and the lost coin. And similarly in the Supper we have a double parable, the parable of the bread and the parable of the wine; though here again, as in other cases, the two are not exactly the same, but the first is shorter and simpler, and the second fuller and richer. And yet there is such an essential similarity between the two as to justify us in bringing them into the closest relation, and employing the one as an aid to the interpretation of the other.

John C. Lambert

147   *BOTH ELEMENTS ARE NEEDED*

To "eat the flesh" and to "drink the blood" of the Son of Man are not the same. The former is to receive the power of self-giving and self-sacrifice to the uttermost. The latter is to receive, in and through that self-giving and self-sacrifice, the life that is triumphant over death and united to God. Both "elements" are needed for the full act of "communion"—which suggests that to receive the holy communion in one kind only is grievously detrimental to the full reality of the sacrament. The life that gives itself even to death; the life that rises from death into union with God: these are the divine gifts without which "ye have not life in yourselves" (John 6:53). But he who receives and makes his own those gifts hath eternal life. For those gifts are true food and drink of men; he who receives them and makes them his own "abideth in me and I in him" (John 6:56).

William Temple

148   *MORE THAN BREAD*

What is the relation between the matter and the Spirit? Which is the bread and which our Lord's body? The relation is the same as between our body and our spirit. The relation is the same, but we have no knowledge, and cannot have, how Christ is related to the bread, but we know he is present in the bread. Christ takes the bread and uses it as his body, to come as a self-conscious body to another self-conscious body, by which means he comes to me, and thank God, I come to him, and we are one, one body and one spirit, Jesus the foundation stone. If we could order our minds on that belief it would help us very much. The sacrament is nothing but Christ, like my body it is nothing, and yet it is everything; the element is nothing; but Christ is everything. We can say with all Protestants that the bread is still bread after the consecration, but to say it is *only* bread is sheer madness and nonsense as it brings us Jesus in our communion.

G. A. Studdert-Kennedy

149   *THE SIMPLICITY OF THE SUPPER*

The simplicity of Christ comes to its crown in the feast of the Lord's Supper. There is no gorgeous rite or showy ceremonial. There is nothing of that many-colored pageantry that had once been needful to attract the world. A cup of wine and a piece of broken bread—these are the seals and symbols of the gospel. And I never feel the simplicity of God and of God's great plan for rescuing the world—I never feel it so powerfully and so freshly as when I sit at the communion table. There are great mysteries in our redemption. There are deep things that even the angels cannot fathom. But in the center is a fact so simple that its best ritual is bread and wine.

George H. Morrison

150   *ATTITUDE OF THE SOUL*

A great many people seem to think that religion is a kind of luxury in life, a Sunday delicacy, an educated taste, an unessential food, which one can, at his discretion, take or go without. But to Jesus Christ religion is no such super-imposed accessory; it is simply bread and water, the daily necessity, the fundamental food, the universally essential and normal satisfaction of the natural hunger and the human thirst. Let us, of all things, hold fast to the naturalness, simplicity and wholesomeness of the religious life. Religion is not a luxury added to the normal life; it is the rational attitude of the soul in its relation to the universe of God. It is not an accident that the central sacrament of the Christian life is the sacrament of daily food and drink.

Francis Greenwood Peabody

151   *THE CONSECRATION OF THE COMMONPLACE*

The fifth century liturgical custom known as "Ordo Romanus Primus" [is] from a much simpler economy, when most people supported themselves by agricultural labor, and when there was little cash money in the average pocket. When families came to holy communion, they brought from home a small flask of homemade wine such as they drank themselves, and a small loaf of bread they had baked for their own tables. This was the offertory. From it, bread and wine were taken for the holy communion itself; some went for the support of the clergy, who lived the same way their people did, and the rest was given to the poor. People brought to church the very things they used to sustain their own lives—the fruit of their own labor. They received it back symbolically as one or two of the loaves were broken and shared in the congregation and one or two of the flasks of wine were poured into the chalice and passed from communicant to communicant. They then returned to the world to go on with the tasks of Christian living.

Charles Duell Kean

E. ON SYMBOLS AND SACRAMENTS

152   *EMBEDDED IN THE DIVINE DEPTH*

A symbol has divine depth in the sense that it refers to a multiple aspect of reality. It is a vehicle which carries past and present meanings; it is suggestive and receptive; it is given and is in the making; it is both form and content, a thing and a sign; it binds the world of things to the world of man's innermost consciousness, and does it by way of an external reference. A symbol is like everything else in the universe—it means beyond itself. The great symbols of tradition are not arbitrary or accidental. They are profoundly embedded in the the divine depth of life where man and God meet.

Samuel H. Miller

153   *POWER OF THE SYMBOLIC*

The power of the symbol lies in its immediacy. It can suggest so much and so instantly and to all simultaneously, and that without elaboration or the distraction which the attempt to say the same thing in words must impose. Take the simplest and most common of symbols, the uplifted hand of benediction, and see how it moves a multitude, imposes a mood, bends all in one emotion, as the wind sweeps a cornfield. Consider how much it summarizes—of God the Father; of the mission of Christ, which in the act re-emerges from the heavens; of the communion of the Spirit; of the forgiveness of sins; of the presence of the supernatural in the church. All of this is implied in benediction, and all who receive the blessing together are aware of it. Or again, how long will it take to say in words what is said by the two bits of stick tied crosswise and set on a soldier's grave? How else could you say it to the passerby and touch every heart? That symbol creates its own atmosphere. It appeals to imagination and to association. It unites. It brings together in time and space—what it means to one it has meant to so many in all the ages— what it means to us it means to men of the one faith the world over. And it has the power of allusion, bringing before the mind on the moment a world of recollection, and places the soul in contact with its beliefs and hopes. It has the short way to the heart. The two sticks on the grave have infinite implications—of sacrifice, redemption, peace, promise for the body—"still united to Christ." Could any inscription say as much, or say it and be felt as all men feel this? Symbol conveys its message without the cumber of mental effort or the challenge to thought which the verbal statement imposes. Hence its restfulness—itself a great value.

H. J. Wotherspoon

154   *MORE THAN MERE SYMBOL*

It is essential to the spiritual of this sacrament that we do what the Lord did. It is all symbol, no doubt, but it is expressive, not arbitrary, symbol; that is to say, the spiritual reality signified is actually conveyed by the symbol. The symbol is emphatically not *mere* symbol; if it were that, we should only receive what our minds could grasp of the meaning symbolized. It is an instrument of the Lord's purpose to give himself to us, as well as the symbol of what he gives. What we receive is not limited by our capacity to understand the gift. When with the right intention I receive the bread and the wine, I actually receive Christ, whether I have any awareness of this at the moment or not, and always more fully than I am aware. We, by repeating and so identifying ourselves with his sacrificial act, become participants in his own sacrifice, which is the perfect dedication to the Father of the humanity which God in Christ has taken to himself.

William Temple

155   *THE HIGHER SACRAMENTALISM OF JESUS*

Physical symbols, and physical contacts, may *occasion* spiritual experience; but they do not *necessarily convey* it. Else were the whole world spiritually minded; and Jesus had never been rejected. . . . The crowd *thronged* Jesus, we read in Mark's Gospel, but one woman in that crowd *touched* him with faith. The grace of God is never an *impartation;* it is always a *gift;* and a gift requires a *receiver.* Two men may see a cross: to one it is a mere "gibbet"; to another it is the symbol of the way by which the world may be "overcome," and, indeed, was "overcome" by Jesus. The window lets in the light, but not to the blind. It reveals the wide-stretching landscape, but not if we close our eyes. Nor is what we see dependent merely upon the window, and upon our physical eyesight: it is dependent on our whole mental and spiritual perceptiveness. The whole universe is sacramental, but only if we are spiritually

awake. This is the higher sacramentalism of the teaching of Jesus. . . .
Not everyone who perceives the outward sign receives the spiritual truth
signified. Not everyone who eats the bread receives the Bread of Life.

C. J. Wright

156   *SACRAMENTAL CHARACTER OF NATURE*

The things of earth are pledges and sacraments of things in heaven.
It is not for nothing that God has selected for his sacraments the com-
monest of all acts—a meal, and the most abundant of all materials, water.
Think you that he means to say that only through two channels his Spirit
streams into the soul? Or is it not much more in unison with his dealings
to say that these two are set apart to signify to us the sacramental
character of all nature? Just as a miracle was intended not to reveal God
working there, at *that* death-bed and in *that* storm, but to call attention to
his presence in *every* death and in *every* storm. Go out at this spring
season of the year; see the mighty preparations for life that nature is
making; feel the swelling sense of gratefulness, and the pervasive ex-
panding consciousness of love for all being; and then say, whether this
whole form which we call nature is not the great sacrament of God, the
revelation of his existence, and the channel of his communications to
the spirit?

Frederick W. Robertson

157   *GOD'S STARTING POINT*

The sacraments, the sacred acts of the church, are impressive enough
just on the basis of their antiquity. When you look in upon the earliest
moments of Christian history, you find them claiming the closest attention and reverence of those first pilgrims in the faith. At the very beginning you discover their common usage. There never was a day when
Christians were without baptism and the Lord's Supper. There were
long years before the Bible was written out in full. The church as we
know it blossomed a good season after the soil had been turned. The
liturgy was the development of long experimental centuries. But right
there at the beginning were the Word and the sacraments. It couldn't be
otherwise. They are God's starting point. And they are inseparable, for
God's Word always comes arm in arm with the sacred act. He never
just talks. And there cannot be, even in smallest measure, a sacred act
without having the "Word" of God in it.

Charles T. Sardeson

158 *PERSONAL CONTACT WITH THE PERSONAL CHRIST*

In the sacraments we are given something which, if it is anything, is straight from God. We escape from the human mediation which in other worship, in the church prayers and in the preacher's disquisition, obstructs almost as often as it helps. Here at last all things are of God. We are busy with God and God with us. Not that grace is more immediate in sacraments than in other ordinances—it is not—but that in sacraments its immediacy is more obvious. To the natural mind there is always reasonable hope that good teaching may on its own merits do good to the hearers, and again that if one asks one may receive—nothing supernatural need in either of these cases be supposed. But from the sacraments nothing is to be expected unless the finger of God is there. In this aspect they may be even considered to be among ordinances distinctively spiritual in the absoluteness of their appeal to and dependence upon faith. They have this religious value, that they testify that God has other ways to the soul than the dialectic. In belief the soul has contact with truth; in conscience it has contact with law; in sacraments it has personal contact with the personal Christ; we see with our eyes, we look upon, our hands handle—at least *of* the Word of Life—and the Life is manifest, and we see and declare it.

H. J. Wotherspoon

159 *THE PROTESTANT SACRAMENTS*

We hold to two sacraments. We do not deny that all of life is sacramental in that it points us to God's handiwork and presence. We do deny that all of life is sacramental in pointing with equal clarity to the saving love of God effected on the cross. Marriage, for example, may be called sacramental in that it points to a "Love divine, all loves excelling," but marriage is not confined to Christian faith, nor does it point to Jesus' death. For that matter, marriage is not given to all Christians. This is why Protestant Christians define as sacraments only those signs given by Jesus himself to all believers, showing and sealing the saving love of God. The two sacraments of baptism and the Lord's Supper declare that life becomes new, not because of anything we do or can do, but because of him who makes all things new. Baptism means that life has been made new—so baptism is not repeated. The Supper means that this new life must continually be sustained and nourished by him who has made it new, that he who has begun a good work in us "will bring it to completion" (Phil. 1:6 RSV).

John Frederick Jansen

160   THE PHYSICAL CONVEYS THE SPIRITUAL

A sacrament I should define as an event in which the material not merely represents but actually conveys the spiritual. It is here, if anywhere, that the term "miracle" will take place. This "miracle" occurs not infrequently in connection with a sermon. Consider what occurs. A created being, not very wise, not very good, and probably very tired, prepares his sermon in his study. When he delivers his sermon, his words are but a physical thing, for they are breath. The sound waves strike upon some hearer's ear, and by some strange, unpredictable, inexplicable concourse by the divine Spirit with the speaker's words, the hearer is aware that the living God is dealing with his soul. It is but the same "miracle" when in the communion service the bread and wine convey to the believing heart that which they are called to represent.

Nathaniel Micklem

161   THE SACRAMENTAL IN THE SACRAMENT

There is little use in any church retaining the sacraments at all, unless it maintains a high, or, to use a worthier word, the Christocentric view of them. As acts of piety, they are not indispensable; as acts of Christ's evangel, they are invaluable. Therefore, if all sacraments are to continue in their place in the church's life, we must maintain and magnify the true evangelical idea that we go there, not—not primarily—because of something we do, which we might, perhaps as well, do elsewhere, but because of what, there, Christ says and does. Not, indeed . . . that Christ says and does the gospel only there. But he says and does it there most personally, most plainly, most intimately to the believing and expectant soul. This is the sacramental in the sacrament.

P. Carnegie Simpson

162   AS GUESTS OF GOD

He commanded the multitude to sit down on the grass, and took the five loaves, and the two fishes, and looking up to heaven, he blessed, and brake, and gave the loaves to his disciples, and the disciples to the multitude.
MATTHEW 14:19

Jesus did not personally give the bread to the multitude—he passed it, as he passes all his bread, through the ministries and servants of his own appointing.

It was more than a mere miracle; it was a sacrament. He made a religious feast of it. He never did anything secularly, as we use that cold term—his whole life was religious, his very breath was a prayer, the opening of his eyes was a revelation. He did nothing without his Father. We should have larger comforts if we had more religion in the using of them. Your unblest bread will soon be done. If you eat animally you will be choked, if you eat sacramentally you will have bread enough and to spare. Eat with contentment of heart, with a sense of gratitude and thankfulness to God, as the guest of God, and the host will see that you have enough.

Joseph Parker

163 *THE EVER-DEEPENING NEED*

As faiths grow ancient, it is increasingly hard to keep the feelings tender. It may grow easier to comprehend, but it does not become easier to adore. And, therefore, the ever-deepening need, when the vision of Christ has passed into the creed, that the heart be quickened, and the affections warmed, and the life of feeling given its own place. . . . God has provided for that need. . . . He has provided for it in the sacraments, where there is so little to satisfy the mind, and yet so much that wins unerringly into the very secret of the soul. For the sacraments lift up as no voice to preach. They move in a realm where argument is silent. They are a simple picture, drawn by the hand of heaven, and such as the eyes of a child delight to dwell upon. And so do they lead us to the childlike spirit, where trust and wonder and love are all-embracing, and where the greatest and most real of things are the things that never can be proved.

George H. Morrison

164 *HEAVENLY MEANINGS*

The particular sacraments are meant to teach us that all life is sacramental. Every deliberate act should be, in a sense, the outward sign of inward grace. A sacrament is more than a symbol. A symbol leads us from the lower to the higher; a sacrament brings us back again to earth, but infuses a heavenly meaning and divine potency into common things and actions.

William R. Inge

F. IN THE BREAKING OF BREAD

165   A NATURAL EXPRESSION OF LOVE

If men were to cast about for a simple and natural ceremony fitted to express a love and admiration for Jesus Christ, nothing more appropriate could suggest itself than the idea of a commemorative meal. Such an idea is in accord with the ways and habits of men. Whenever men lay aside the toils of common life to come gladly and willingly together for purposes of intellectual or sentimental fellowship, they gather, if possible, around a friendly board. . . . In the earliest ages of mankind the feast lent itself to sacramental uses. Human nature has not changed; and the banquet, on varying scales, continues to fulfill the function of a commemorative and uniting action. . . . Had our Master himself not created the religious banquet called the Lord's Supper, something distantly approaching it would doubtless have been invented by Christian piety.

Robert M. Adamson

166   THE CUSTOM OF THE COMMON MEAL

The view has been put forward in recent years, and there is much to be said for it, that the ordinance of the Lord's Supper had a twofold root. It commemorated the supper which Jesus had held with his disciples on the eve of his death, but this had been only the last of many similar meals which were well remembered. Jesus had been accustomed to close the day with a simple repast, at which he conversed freely with his companions; and it was on these occasions, more than on any others, that they had come near to him and learned to know him. In after days they associated him most vividly with these common meals. This would seem to be the suggestion in the story of the journey to Emmaus, when the two disciples failed to recognize their fellow-traveler until they began a meal with him and knew him as he distributed the bread (Luke 24:31). These words can have no reference to the Last Supper, for the two disciples are described as outside the circle of the twelve. But all who were on terms of friendship with Jesus were familiar with his characteristic actions at the evening meals at which they had sometimes been present.

After his death it was only natural that his followers should maintain the practice of a common supper, and this is expressly mentioned in a significant notice in the book of Acts: "They continued . . . in the fellowship, and in breaking of bread" (Acts 2:42). Jesus was no longer with them, but they could not take part in the accustomed meal without remembering how he had formerly presided at it. They believed that he was still invisibly present, and with the ordinary meal they combined a brief ceremony re-enacting what he had done and said at the Last Supper. In this theory there is much that is attractive, and it offers a natural explanation of how the supper came to be adopted as a standing ordinance. In a manner it already bore his character. The disciples merely perpetuated the custom which Jesus had taught them, and around this custom the Christian society grew.

Ernest F. Scott

167   *FOUNDATION OF THE CHURCH*

On his last evening, Jesus had gathered his disciples together for a supper. Only ceremonial meals were eaten at the beginning of the night; the customary hour for the main meal was earlier. . . . It became a farewell meal. For during the supper Jesus took a flat, round loaf of bread, broke it, as one usually did with bread, and divided the portions of the one loaf among his disciples. In the same way after supper, since goblets with wine were standing on the table, he had one of these goblets passed around among them, and each disciple drank from it. Any man of the ancient world, or any primitive man, would have understood the meaning of such an act even without accompanying words: the disciples were to feel themselves to be a fellowship, just as they had already been while they journeyed, ate and drank with the Master. For eating together binds the partakers of the meal one to another. . . . Separation from the Master is what confronts this circle, but they are to remain united, even without him, until the day when the table fellowship is renewed in the Kingdom of God. This is his foundation. Even if Jesus had not spoken of his death, he did nevertheless establish this independent fellowship. The Last Supper signifies the foundation of the church.

Martin Dibelius

168   *MEAL OF MEMORIES*

The "breaking of bread" was the distinctive act of worship of the first believers. It was a continuation of the table fellowship which the original disciples had enjoyed with Jesus. Though he was no longer with them in the flesh, they could celebrate together the simple meal at which he had once presided in person. It was a meal which brought back memories of the times when he had broken the bread to distribute to them. Especially they would recall the Last Supper "on the same night in which he was betrayed" (1 Cor. 11:23). But the spirit in which they partook of the meal was not one of sadness or sorrow. They broke bread "with gladness and singleness of heart" (Acts 2:46). Their eyes were fixed on the banquet of the Kingdom of God. Jesus had promised to drink with them anew at that time. Perhaps he would return at some celebration of the "breaking of bread."

Clarence Tucker Craig

169   *THE REVELATION OF THE INSIGNIFICANT*

He took the bread . . . and their eyes were opened.   LUKE 24:30-31, RV

It was in no sense a sacramental meal, as we use that word sacrament in our theology. It was a frugal supper in a village home of two tired travelers, and Another. Yet it was then—in the breaking of the bread, and not in any vision of resurrection splendor—that they knew that their companion was the Lord. How that discovery flashed upon their hearts, the Bible, so wonderful in its silences, does not tell. It may have been the quiet air of majesty with which he took at once the place of host, when they had invited him in to be their guest. It may have been the familar word of blessing that awakened sweet memories of Galilean days. Or it may have been that as he put forth his hand after the blessing to take the bread and break it, they saw that it was a hand which had been pierced. However it was, whether by word or hand, they felt irresistibly that this was he. Some little action, some dear familiar trait, told them in a flash this was the Christ. . . . In daily life we are always meeting that— the revelation of the insignificant.

George H. Morrison

170   *THE BROTHERHOOD OF THE BURNING HEART*

The "breaking of bread" was instituted to be a heartening service for discouraged disciples in their sadness and disappointments. Jesus foresaw sorrowful hearts going to Emmaus, many discouraged souls despondent by backsets to some fond hopes, and provided a table where love may find response to spiritual aspirations. He was known in the breaking of bread, and the recognition brought instant satisfaction, and removed every contradiction and doubt. That recognized presence gave new strength for new duties, so that with changed purpose the two obscure disciples immediately became missionaries of the resurrection gospel. It has ever been that when the heart burns, the sacred fire can maintain itself only by going to kindle other hearts. "They rose up the same hour, and returned to Jerusalem" (Luke 24:33). Ever since the breaking of bread is a love-feast, which belongs to the brotherhood of the burning heart.

David Owen Thomas

171   THE SIMPLICITY OF TABLE FELLOWSHIP

This Emmaus episode tells exactly how the disciples recognized their walking companion as the risen Christ. The simple, everyday nature of the event, so utterly like the simplicity of him whom they had known during his ministry as their table companion, is filled with significance for future generations of Christians who would know Christ in the celebration of the Lord's Supper. Here is a point of transition from the everyday companionship at meals and the solemnization of this fellowship on the night before his death to the church as the mystical body of Christ. The church is constituted in the confessions of many churches by the preaching of the word of God and by the celebration of the gospel sacraments. The simple naturalness of the event at Emmaus suggests at once the need for keeping the future ecclesiastical responses always in close association with these simple acts of table fellowship, lest they develop into specialized religious institutions, no longer pointing to their origins, but becoming sacred mechanisms with a false independence of their own.

William J. Wolf

G. THIS DO IN REMEMBRANCE

172   *SPIRIT OF EXPECTANCY*

It is because we forget what our Lord was so anxious we should keep
in remembrance that we find a sacrament so uninspiring. We are so
intent upon what we and others have come to do that we forget that One
whom we cannot see with the eyes of flesh is present to do something
for us. A. E. W. Mason says of Francis Drake that he always looked
out on life as though he expected doors to open before him through
which he would pass to magic realms and great experiences. . . . It is
that spirit of expectancy that matters in spiritual things as in everything
else.

Roderick Bethune

173   *HEAVEN IN THE HEART*

Men become like the thoughts they harbor, like the memories they
cherish. Whatever a man's mental life is, is bound to affect his trans-
actional life. It is the veriest truth that "as [a man] thinketh in his heart,
so is he" (Prov. 23:7). As we entertain bad thoughts, our own character
becomes bad, cheap and common. As we hold high and holy memories,
our lives are made strong and beautiful and great. To remember him,
to cherish the thought of him, is to harbor heaven in your heart. It is not
what the swift sweep of thought bears over the mind that enriches or im-
poverishes, but the deposit that memory holds; and when Christ would
bless the world, he bade it think of, aye, *remember* him, for what we
remember really blesses, as what we save and not what we earn enriches.
He knew what nineteen hundred years have taught and experience has
tested, that he, the personal Christ, was best worthy of remembrance,
and they who remember him most become most like him, and therefore
best.

Henry Hitt Crane

174   *REMEMBERING CHRIST*

It must be profitable for us to recall, as we sit before this table, the
life of this great Friend of ours, the words of wisdom and gentleness that

he spoke, the great truths that he made plain to us, the gracious ministry of help and healing and sympathy to which his life was given, the patience with which he bore the spite and scorn and violence of the brutal men whom he sought to bless, the unresisting meekness with which he went to death, conquering hate by enduring it, and winning in his death the contrite love of the men who slew him. To spend an hour, now and then, in simply recalling all that we know about him, in meditating upon this character, in comparing our own habitual thinking and living with this standard, must be a profitable exercise for every one of us.

Washington Gladden

175 *REMEMBERED IN HIS DEATH*

What he chose to be remembered for is significant. He was famous for his teaching, and yet more notable for his wondrous works. Yet he chose neither. He would be remembered in his death. That was because his death was no ordinary martyrdom. He gave his life a ransom for many. His death was a propitiatory sacrifice for the sin of the world. Into the world of sin, divine forgiveness came by divine love itself bearing, before our eyes, our sins or their results. In the death of Christ, as in nothing else, we see the awfulness of sin, and are brought to acknowledge the penalty that is due. There, as nowhere else, the pain and the shame of sin are awakened. In the supreme moment of forgiveness, we find that forgiveness is made possible because at last we have seen sin with the eyes of God. It was this that the Lord would bring constantly to our remembrance.

Charles Fiske

176 *WHAT TO REMEMBER*

Jesus was asking his disciples to remember him . . . as one who found a place in history. There in their land and then in their time he had lived, moved and had his being. God had been so richly present in him that they came to believe that he was the heaven-sent Messiah, but this was not to obscure the prior fact that this incredible being was one of themselves. His village was known, his family was known, his years of quiet labor in Joseph's carpenter shop were known. Remember me, Jesus might have said, and discover in history the true meaning of existence. In me you can glimpse a new dimension for your own lives and for all mankind.

In the second place, Jesus was asking them to remember him as the center of their communal life. He was the vine, they were the branches. Their lives were inextricably united. But they did not live unto themselves. The most important thing about this vine was its caretaker. God was the husbandman. He expected it to bear fruit. He stripped off the sterile branches. He pruned those that bore fruit so that they would bear a larger crop. "If you abide in me, and my words abide in you, ask whatever you will and it shall be done for you" (John 15:7). They were the church of the living God, the community of the faithful, the living organism through which the life of heaven flowed to mankind.

Harold E. Fey

177   *WE ARE THERE*

In the eucharist the church perpetually reconstructs the crisis in which the Kingdom of God came in history. It never gets beyond this. At each eucharist we are *there*—we are in the night in which he was betrayed, at Golgotha, before the empty tomb on Easter Day, and in the upper room where he appeared; and we are at the moment of his coming with angels and archangels and all the company of heaven, in the twinkling of an eye, at the last trump. Sacramental communion is not a purely mystical experience to which history, as embodied in the form and matter of the sacrament, would be, in the last resort, irrelevant. It is bound up with a corporate memory of real events. History has been taken up into the supra-historical without ceasing to be history.

C. H. Dodd

178   *THE DOOR TO GOD*

Here the church from the beginning has realized that Presence which is the source of her life and power, has expressed her adoration, thanksgiving and penitence, has made her supplications for the living and the dead, offered her oblation, received the food of immortality, and remembered the prevailing sacrifice from which her life began. And here, in spite of periodical relapses towards primitive conceptions, corruption, slackness, grave conflict of theory, and many bewildering divergences of practice, the Christian can still find the same essential sources of worship, refreshment and inwardness; the same access to the inexhaustible Divine Charity, and the same invitation to oblation and communion in the offering and hallowing of bread and wine. Even were we to set aside the sacred character of its historic origin and its supernatural claim, no other rite could so well embody the homely and transcendental paradox of Christianity: the universal divine action, and the intimate divine approach to every soul; the food of daily life, and the mystery of eternal life, both given at once; the historical memorial perpetually renewed, yet finding its fulfilment in a real and enduring Presence unfettered by the categories of time and space. Here the most naive worshipper finds an invitation to love and gratitude, and a focus for his devotion, which he can apprehend though never explain; and the contemplative finds a door which opens upon the ineffable mystery of God. Those deep levels of our being which live unchanged under the flow of outward life, and of which we sometimes become aware—those levels where we thirst for God and apprehend him, and know our truest selves to consist in a certain kinship with him—these levels are reached and stirred by the movement of the eucharist.

Evelyn Underhill

H. RITE OF THE COVENANT

179   *LAST NIGHT OF THE OLD COVENANT*

The night of the betrayal was the last night of the old covenant, and everything in the paschal celebration was arranged to recall the memorable birth-night of the nation. That was the greatest night in human history, not only because it celebrated the ransom of Israel from imminent death and their emancipation from slavery, but because it was the night of the world's greatest gloom and darkness, and ushered in a new day, for with the day of the new covenant Jesus brought life and immortality to light. While the communion reminds us of the night of the betrayal and the death of the cross, through faith it graciously assures us that the night is over and that the "Sun of righteousness" is risen, for believers are "the children of light" (John 12:36).

David Owen Thomas

180   *THE COVENANT OF GRACE*

There is in the Lord's Supper a mutual solemn profession of the two parties transacting the covenant of grace, and visibly united in that covenant; the Lord Christ by his minister, on the one hand, and the communicants (who are professing believers) on the other. . . . Christ presents himself to the believing communicants as their propitiation and bread of life. . . . And they in receiving what is offered . . . profess to embrace the promises and to lay hold of the hope set before them, to receive the atonement, to receive Christ as their spirtual food, and to feed upon him in their hearts by faith. Indeed, what is professed on both sides is the *heart;* for Christ in offering himself professes the willingness of *his heart* to be theirs who duly receive him; all the communicants, on their part, profess the willingness of *their hearts* to receive him. . . . Thus the Lord's Supper is plainly a *mutual* renovation, confirmation, and seal of the covenant of grace: both the covenanting parties profess their consent to their respective parts in the covenant of grace.*

Jonathan Edwards

181 *FULFILMENT OF PROPHECY*

This cup means the new covenant ratified by my blood shed for your sake. LUKE 22:20 (MOFFATT)

This indicates that under the form of the cup or of the wine within the cup the "new covenant" is given and appropriated. "New covenant" takes us back to Jeremiah 31:31, but as a new covenant necessarily presupposes an older one the roots of the conception stretch still farther back to the ancient covenant which God made with Israel at the Exodus (Ex. 24:4-8). The the new covenant like its prototype is instituted by sacrifice appears by the explanatory addition, "ratified by my blood shed for your sake." Jesus is conscious that through the shedding of his blood the new covenant of which prophecy spoke becomes for his followers an accomplished fact into the benefits of which they now proleptically enter. His death is not a tragedy simply or a price demanded by fidelity to a cause. It is the means of bringing on, instituting, applying, and sealing a redemption which by his life and word he has sought to effect but which only the final sacrifice of his life will bring to fulfilment. Thus Jesus, according to the evangelical tradition, reads the final purpose of God in his own mysterious fortunes.

The Lord's Supper as thus presented indicates and inaugurates a redemption effected by the death of Christ as a sacrifice. "Christ knew that his death was at hand. But he believed that by his death the disciples would be saved from the world as were the Israelites from Egypt" (Easton). The rite points to this final redemption; it expresses the solidarity of the disciples with Christ; and it perpetuates the memorial of the sacrifice by which the redemption is won.

William Manson

182 *CHALICE OF OBEDIENCE*

Now at length we are drawing near to the blood-red center of his passion, the heart of the inner experience of Jesus. His costly deed of sacrifice rose up before his vision in the sacred symbol of "the cup." "My cup" he called it in his interview with the ambitious sons of Zebedee (Mark 10:39)—"the cup that I shall drink of" (Matt. 20:22). It was "his portion," his "lot" in life, assigned to him by the will and providence of God. And at the Last Supper when he took the cup he said "this is my blood of the [new] covenant, which is shed for many" (Mark 14:24

RV). Out of the Father's vineyard the wine of the ripe fruit was to be pressed at last in the wine-press of Israel's pride and hate and scorn—the wine press of the divine agony. And it was in the death upon the cross that all the forth-flowing holy energy of God—the very law of whose being is sacrifice—was to be pressed in one distilled and concentrated blood-red draught of forgiveness. The golden chalice was the love of Jesus held in the grasp of a perfect obedience.

James A. Robertson

I. HE LAID DOWN HIS LIFE

183   CHRIST'S PLEDGE OF PARDON AND LOVE

The Lord's table is the trysting-place between the Savior and the sinner. It is here that we receive the assurance of the divine forgiveness of all our sins. It is that same love, sore wounded but undaunted and unflinching, that we see coming to us in the sacrament. We hear him say to us, as he takes the cup: "Drink ye all of it; for this is my blood of the new testament, which is shed for many for the remission of sins" (Matt. 26:27-28). It is made plain to the simplest mind that Christ's sacrificial death is linked up with the forgiveness of sin. As old Rabbi Duncan said to the poor fallen woman who wept at the table and hesitated to take the cup into her hands, "Take it, take it, woman, it's for *sinners*." And when we do take him at his word, we are united with him in his Spirit, and we are released from the guilt and power of sin. In the holy communion, Christ puts into our hands this pledge of overflowing pardon and love. Thus he heals our sorrows and our wounds. "Let us consider, then" (as the old Exhortation of 1560 says) "that his sacrament is a singular medicine for all poor sick creatures, a comfortable help to weak souls, and that our Lord requireth no other worthiness on our part, but that we unfeignedly acknowledge our naughtiness and imperfection."

Philip W. Lilley

184   INTERPRETING THE LORD'S DEATH

The rite of the Supper . . . is of use to *interpret* the Lord's death. It throws important light on the meaning of that solemn event. The institution of this symbolic feast was in fact the most important contribution made by Jesus during his personal ministry to the doctrine of the atonement through the sacrifice of himself. Therefore more clearly than from any other act or word performed or spoken by him, the twelve might learn to conceive of their Master's death as possessing a *redemptive* character. Thereby Jesus, as it were, said to his disciples: My approaching passion is not to be regarded as a mere calamity, or dark disaster, falling out contrary to the divine purpose or my expectation; not as a fatal blow inflicted by ungodly men on me and you, and the cause which is dear to us all; not even as an evil which may be overruled for good; but as an event fulfilling, not frustrating, the purpose of my mission, and fruitful of blessing to the world. What men mean for evil, God means for good, to bring to pass to save much people alive. The shedding of my blood, in one aspect the crime of the wicked Jews, is in another aspect my own voluntary act. I pour forth my blood for a gracious end, even for the remission of sins. My death will initiate a new dispensation, and seal a new testament; it will fulfil the purpose, and therefore take the place, of the manifold sacrifices of the Mosaic ritual, and in particular of the paschal lamb, which is even now being eaten. I shall be the Paschal Lamb of the Israel of God henceforth; at once protecting them from death, and feeding their souls with my crucified humanity, as the bread of eternal life.

Alexander Balmain Bruce

185   THE ETERNAL ACT REPRESENTED

For us the holy communion is a sacrifice—that of ourselves, our souls and bodies, which we thereby consecrate to the service of God. It is a commemoration of a sacrifice—that of Christ upon the cross. It is also the representation of a sacrifice—that of the Son of God regarded as an eternal act. With reference to the last, we may say, if we like, using popular language, that we are doing on earth what Christ is doing in heaven. We are certainly right to insist that the sacrifice on Calvary has its eternal and therefore ever-active side; but we must remember that it is the eternal act that we are symbolically representing, not the temporal act that we are repeating or continuing, when we celebrate the eucharist.

William R. Inge

186   THE CHURCH'S SACRIFICE

The eucharist is a sacrifice because in it the Christian church—the great priestly body and "soul of the world"—exercises her privilege of sonship in free approach to the Father in the name of Christ. She comes before the Father with her material offerings of bread and wine, and of those things wherein God has prospered her, bearing witness that all good things come from him; and though he needs nothing from man, yet he accepts the recognition of his fatherhood from loyal and free hearts. She comes with her wide-spreading intercessions for the whole race of

mankind, and for her members living and departed. She offers her glad
sacrifice of praise and thanksgiving for all the blessings of creation and
redemption. She solemnly commemorates the passion in word and in
symbolic action, through the bread broken and the wine outpoured, the
appointed tokens of Christ's sacrificed body and blood, reciting before
God his own words and acts in instituting the holy eucharist. This is the
church's sacrifice; and it is all that she can do. She can but make the
appointed remembrance of Christ's passion and death and resurrection
and of his second coming which she awaits, and offer to the Father the
appointed symbols, praying him by the consecrating power of the Holy
Ghost to fill the sacrifice with a divine power by accepting the earthly
elements at the heavenly altar.

Charles Gore

187   *MADE SACRED THROUGH LOVE*

Christ chose one of the most ordinary acts of human life—the evening
meal—and by filling it with his spirit of tenderness, love, and self-
sacrifice, made it beautiful; forever dear and poetic to the hearts of men.
It was a representative act. He did not mean by it that this act was holy
and this alone, or was specially holy—but in making this common act
sacred through the spirit of love with which he did it with them, he en-
shrined the principle that all natural, unselfish acts are sacred and beautiful; all human doing is divine which is done in the same spirit as that in
which he took with them the bread and wine. So, where we have the heart
of Christ, no act is common or unclean; no work worldly, no profession
secular, no busines undivine. The spirit of pure unselfish love sanctifies
all labor. God's love in man makes lovely every act. The heart of sacrifice makes all action sacramental.

Stopford A. Brooke

188   *THE WORD WHICH RALLIED THEM*

As baptism marked Jesus' entry into his earthly ministry, so the institution of the supper marked the consummation of it. It was his last act in
the midst of his disciples while with them in the flesh. The final conflict
with the prince of this world was at hand. The faith of the disciples was
crumbling. In a few short hours all understanding and all obedience
would be carried away in the flood of disaster. They would all forsake
him, and he would have to go forward utterly alone to make the final

offering of obedience on behalf of all men, and win on behalf of all men the final battle. At that moment, when all faith was crumbling, he staked all upon a deed. He took bread and wine, told them, "This is my body . . . given for you. . . . This . . . is . . . my blood . . . shed for you. . . . This do in remembrance of me" (Luke 22:19-20), and then went out to suffer and die alone. And on the first Lord's Day, when the victory was won, but the disciples were defeated and broken, it was in the breaking of the bread that he was made known to them in his risen power. When all landmarks were submerged in the flood of disaster, and stories of his resurrection seemed but an idle tale, it was this utterly simple word, "Do this," which rallied them, and gave them the place at which the meaning of what had happened could be made plain. And thereafter it was in this fellowship at the Lord's table, in the breaking of the bread and the sharing of the cup as he had commanded, that they were made actual participants in his body and his blood, becoming members incorporate in his risen life by participation in his dying.

Lesslie Newbigin

189 *COMMUNICATION OF CHRIST'S LOVE*

Jesus in instituting the Lord's Supper has simply made universal the communication of his sacrificial love. He has made the bread and wine forever, and to all who receive it, the symbol of the life he lived and the death he suffered in love to all mankind. In itself, it is mere bread and wine. Translated by the intelligent and devout recipient into terms of the love and sacrifice it is intended to express, it becomes the bread of life and the wine of love to as many as receive it in this faith. Being an objective institution, coming at stated times and places, it is independent of the wayward caprice, the fickle mood, the listless mind of the individual. And so it calls us back from our worldliness, deepens our penitence, quickens our love, and intensifies our consecration; and, above all, identifies us with the great company of our fellow Christians, as no mere subjective devotion and private prayer could ever do.

William DeWitt Hyde

190 *PERSONAL INVOLVEMENT*

How great the difference between contemplating the cross of our Lord, being a spectator of it, even though it be a very earnest spectator anxious to learn from it, and apprehending in it the activity of his mighty spirit of holiness and love towards mankind and therefore towards *you*. Apprehending that, you cease to be a spectator and become involved in a tremendous and most critical personal relationship. From being a merely solemnizing and subduing spectacle it becomes a crisis, an inescapable challenge from the Christ to *you*. . . . In like manner there is great difference between coming to that central rite of the church which celebrates the death of the Lord with the thought that thus *we* symbolically express certain noble and final truths concerning God and the real values of life, and coming to it with the thought that in some real sense we are to be present, as in the body itself, at that first supper-table and to hear as though it were directly said to our own ears, as though also he were looking into our eyes as he did into the eyes of Peter and James and John, "Take, eat: this is my body, which is broken for you" (1 Cor. 11:24).

Herbert H. Farmer

J. GOD'S ACTION—AND OURS

191   *THE RICHNESS OF GOD'S NATURE*

Communion is a summing up of the whole of worship in one action, that of eating bread and drinking wine together, and that action is a means of remembering both God's work and his nature. It sums up for us his threefold work: of creation, because the elements represent the fruits of the earth; of redemption, because they represent still more the life of Jesus given on the cross; and of sanctification, because the consuming of them represents the coming of God to dwell within us. It brings home to us, in a way that is remarkable for any one symbol, something of the richness and paradox of God's nature; combining the homeliness that we associate with a meal made up of the common things of earth with a sense of the mystery and infinity of God's dealings with us, a feeling that is inevitably brought home to us by a symbol that reaches out into such a multiplicity of rich meanings.

J. Alan Kay

192   *SPIRITUAL DRAMA*

Goethe once said, "The highest cannot be spoken; it can only be acted." This is true of human love at its best. The love of a mother for a child cannot be put into words. It is acted through the long years of affectionate and devoted care. Even so the love of Christ who, "while we were yet sinners . . . died for us" (Rom. 5:8), cannot be expressed in words. Since words and thoughts fail us, we gather up the mystery of it in the communion service, in a spiritual drama: "For as often as ye eat this bread, and drink this cup, ye do shew the Lord's death till he come" (1 Cor. 11:26).

R. Guy Ramsay

193   *THEIR CHARACTER AS ACTS*

The emphasis on the visible character of the sacraments has tended to obscure their character as acts. . . . Action rather than visibility is a more comprehensive description of the character of the sacraments. The sacra-

ments are divine actions, acts of God, of Christ, of the Holy Spirit; they
are acts of the church of Jesus Christ; they call for action from those who
receive them—not only the act of faith but also the "external" and
"public" actions of being baptized, of taking and eating and drinking.
They are actions which are intelligible actions (for they include the Word
—the words of institution and the words of promise). Yet they are also
concrete actions which are not only spiritual but physical as well.

Elmer J. F. Arndt

194   *GOD TAKES ACTION*

Always the Central Figure in a sacrament is God, or, if you prefer so
to put it, the Lord Jesus Christ. And every single time a sacrament is
celebrated, God takes action, there and then—does something, not on
Calvary, but in that church. And what he does is to come to each soul
partaking in the sacrament and to assure it that he stands to the best and
biggest of his promises and to the fullness of his grace in Christ; that it is
still all true for it de-universalizes the Scriptures, and individualizes
them, makes them a personal promise, couched no longer in general
terms, but offered to very you, and very me, as individually as if they
covered no other, but referred to you and me alone. We may be cold
and dead and unresponsive. None the less, something happens in the
sacrament. For God stands to his side of the covenant, whether we stand
to ours or not; is there, making his offer, pressing it upon us, assuring us
we can rely upon it absolutely.

Arthur John Gossip

195   *THE GREAT ACTION*

Adoration, which is the purest form of worship and the most selfless
of human emotions, initiates action. The soul in adoration is lifted out of
self into Christ but cannot be in Christ without his vision and mission
and commission. So the imperative, "Go ye," is inherent in worship at
its core. Worship is man's response to God. We love because he first
loved us. In the holy communion—*the great action*—is this sequence
most evident. Our Lord "took . . . blessed . . . brake . . . gave." Then
he said, "This do."

The Roman Catholics name the holy communion, "Mass," from the
last words used in the Roman Missal, *Ite, missa est.* . . . What do these
words mean? "Go, you are sent forth!" . . . Holy communion does not

---

end with the blessing; it goes with you out the door of the church into the activities of all life.

T. T. Faichney

196   *THE SACRAMENTAL COMMITTAL*

That good thing which was committed unto thee keep by the Holy Ghost which dwelleth in us. 2 TIMOTHY 1:14

The Apostle has uttered his magnificent personal faith that he knows whom he has believed. The basis of his confidence is that he has made full surrender to the will and love of God. He has given himself: body, soul and spirit; his life, past, present and future; as a trust, the security for which is the character of the Trustee. He has handed over all he has and it is as a deposit, which he is confident God will guard. "I . . . am persuaded that he is able to keep that which I have committed unto him against that day" (2 Tim. 2:12). He is in his gracious and faithful keeping, and all must be well.

This, too, is our sacramental committal. By sign and symbol God offers his great love to us in Christ Jesus; and we commit ourselves to it. Our confidence is not in ourselves, but in him, in his power and desire to save and keep and hold and guard. . . . We take the bread and wine as seals attesting his promises and confirming his love. Not upon us but upon him is the burden: not in us but unto him be the glory. A frank and full and free committal is what our sacrament implies on our part.

Hugh Black

197   *GIVEN TO BE RECEIVED*

The consecrated elements are quite truly and certainly a vehicle of Christ's presence to our souls. That presence is given under a form which at once indicates that it is given to be received. Any other use of it seems to me both unauthorized and dangerous. It is dangerous because it suggests that the value of the sacrament is intended to reside in itself. But this is not so. The presence is given to be received; when received it incorporates us into the body of Christ, so that in the power of his eternal sacrifice we may take our allotted share therein, "filling up what is lacking of the sufferings of Christ for his body's sake, which is the church" (Col. 1:24). The proof that we have received the presence is the increase of love in our daily lives. . . . If a man goes out from his communion to love and serve men better he has received the Real Presence. If he feels every thrill and tremor of devotion, but goes out as selfish as before, he has not received it. It was offered, but he did not receive it.

William Temple

198 *RECEIVED AND DELIVERED*

Nothing is really our own until we communicate it to others. We never see these great things until they are on the way to our neighbor. There are birds which never reveal the beauty of their plumage until they lift their wings to fly. And God's wonderful gifts to our spirit, gifts of truth and consolation, nestling in the depths of the soul, never unfold their hidden glory until we disturb them and send them away to other lives. Just when we are giving them away they become ours in unsuspected strength and beauty. I suppose that the Apostle Paul found new insight into the sacred mysteries of the Lord's Supper every time he unveiled its privileges to other people, and led them to the wonderful feast. "I have received of the Lord that which also I delivered unto you" (1 Cor. 11:23). That is the appointed order in all vital possession. We receive of the Lord; we deliver unto you. And it is only in delivering unto others that the wealth of the reception is revealed. Every time Paul brought a new guest to share the sacramental meal his own spiritual inheritance broadened from glory to glory.

John Henry Jowett

K. FELLOWSHIP OF FAITH

199   *INNER UNITY OF FELLOWSHIP*

To maintain the inner unity of fellowship, the [early] Christian group had one instrument by far more potent than any other, the regular celebration of the eucharist. In many respects, Christian worship appears to have developed out of that of the synagogue; this, the eucharistic feast, was the one unique and irreplaceable element. Participation in it was the sign of Christian fellowship; exclusion from it was the most serious penalty that could be imposed on the erring brother. Whatever the peril, whatever the difficulty, and for slaves the difficulty must sometimes have been almost unsurmountable, it was regarded as obligatory for the Christian to be present and to receive the Bread of Life. In private houses, in catacombs, often before the break of day, the Christians assembled, to do what the Lord had appointed, to be fashioned anew into one bread, one body, to be set again firmly within that eternal redemption which God was accomplishing through his risen Christ. So essential was it that every member should be partaker of the "medicine of immortality" that portions from the one loaf were sent to those who were sick, and in time of persecution to those in prison.

Stephen Neill

200   *A FELLOWSHIP OF FAITH*

They continued stedfastly in the . . . fellowship. ACTS 2:42

The greatest thing about the early Christians was not their wealth. For the most part they were poor. They were not distinguished for their scholastic training. Most of them were unlettered. They were not known for their high social position in the Roman world. Most of them belonged to the working class. There was one distinguishable characteristic by which they were known—fellowship. Pentecost had separated these early disciples of Jesus Christ into a church and bound them together in an unbreakable fellowship. On Pentecost it was said of them that "they were all with one accord in one place" (Acts 2:1). It is comparatively easy to get Christians in one place, but to get them in one place "with one accord" is difficult. The fellowship of the early Christians was a fellowship of faith. Not only did they belong to something; they believed something. Their fellowship was a fellowship of suffering. Every footprint in the book of Acts is stained with blood. Nothing happened easily. Their fellowship was a fellowship of prayer. They advanced on their knees. Prayer is mentioned twenty-nine times in the book of Acts. And also their fellowship was a fellowship of love. They possessed the compassionate heart. They cared. They provided for the widows and orphans. They fed the hungry. They were so different from those about them that they were looked upon as a third race. They were a fellowship.

Jesse M. Bader

201   THE CHRISTIAN FELLOWSHIP

In the New Testament *koinōnia* occurs some eighteen times. When we examine the connections in which it is used we come to see how wide and far-reaching is the fellowship which should characterize the Christian life.

In the Christian life there is a *koinōnia* which means "a sharing of friendship" and an abiding in the company of others (Acts 2:42; 2 Cor. 6:14). It is very interesting to note that the friendship is based on common Christian knowledge (1 John 1:3). Only those who are friends with Christ can really be friends with each other.

In the Christian life there is a *koinōnia* which means "practical sharing" with those less fortunate. Paul three times uses the word in connection with the collection he took from his churches for the poor saints at Jerusalem (Rom. 15:26; 2 Cor. 8:4; 2 Cor. 9:13; *cf.* Heb. 13:16). The Christian fellowship is a *practical* thing.

In the Christian life there is a *koinōnia* which is a "partnership in the work of Christ" (Phil. 1:5). Paul gives thanks for the partnership of the Philippians in the work of the gospel.

In the Christian life there is a *koinōnia* "in the faith." The Christian is never an isolated unit; he is one of a believing company (Eph. 3:9).

In the Christian life there is a "fellowship" (*koinōnia*) "in the Spirit" (2 Cor. 13:14; Phil. 2:1). The Christian lives in the presence, the company, the help and the guidance of the Spirit.

In the Christian life there is a *koinōnia* "with Christ." Christians are called to the *koinōnia* of Jesus Christ, the Son of God (1 Cor. 1:9). That fellowship is found specially through the sacrament (1 Cor. 10:16). The cup and the bread are supremely the *koinōnia* of the body and blood of Christ. In the sacrament above all Christians find Christ and find each other. Further, that fellowship with Christ is fellowship with his sufferings (Phil. 3:10). When the Christian suffers he has, amidst the pain, the joy of knowing that he is sharing things with Christ.

In the Christian life there is *koinōnia* "with God" (1 John 1:3). But it is to be noted that that fellowship is ethically conditioned, for it is not for those who have chosen to walk in darkness (1 John 1:6).

The Christian *koinōnia* is that bond which binds Christians to each other, to Christ and to God.

William Barclay

202   *ACTUAL FELLOWSHIP*

Sacramental fellowship is an actual fellowship with a concrete, actual congregation of Christian people. It is a fellowship of mutual service as well as common worship. No more than fellowship with Christ is separable from fellowship with his church is fellowship with others separable from actual fellowship, being together with them and in actual union with them. Such actuality or concreteness belongs to the essence of sacramental fellowship just as the sacraments are inseparable from the ministry of the church. Yet it is also profoundly true that this or that particular, local fellowship does not exhaust the fellowship offered in the sacraments and witnessed to by them. . . . "We who are many"—many individuals, many congregations, many historical churches—are "one body." The one fellowship—so broken, incomplete and even perverse in our concrete historical situation—extends beyond the limits of history to the eternal and perfect fellowship of Christ and his saints. Nonetheless, the fellowship in our concrete situation is real; and its reality —imperfect, indeed—is the earnest of its perfect consummation in eternity.

Elmer J. F. Arndt

203   *THE BOND OF CHARITY*

Let us come to holy communion in charity with each other and with all; determined henceforth to feel for each other, and with each other; to put ourselves in our neighbors' places; to see with their eyes, and to feel with their hearts, so far as God shall give us that great grace; determined to make allowances for their mistakes and failings; to give and forgive, each as God gives and forgives, forever; that so we may be indeed the children of our Father in heaven, whose name is Love.

Charles Kingsley

204   *THE QUAKER TESTIMONY*

Some knew this penetration of spirit [with the presence of God] as a daily illumination. Others, who dare not claim so much for their individual vision, have yet often known the joy of communion where, Christ in our midst, we are made one in the fellowship of power and of overcoming love. This real presence lies at the heart of life. The Quaker community, in all its work and activity, is driven back for power and for guidance to this touch of the living God. In silence, without rite or symbol, we have known the Spirit of Christ so convincingly present in our quiet meetings that his grace dispels our faithlessness, our unwillingness, our fears and sets our hearts aflame with the joy of adoration. We have thus felt the power of the Spirit renewing and recreating our love and friendship for all our fellows. This is our eucharist and our communion.

London Yearly Meeting (1928)

205   *From THE PILGRIM'S PROGRESS*

Then said Christian to the Porter, Sir, what house is this? and may I lodge here to-night? The Porter answered, This house was built by the Lord of the Hill, and he built it for the relief and security of Pilgrims. . . . Now I saw in my Dream that thus they sat talking together until supper was ready. So when they had made ready, they sat down to meat. Now the Table was furnished with fat things, and with Wine that was well refined: and all their talk at the Table was about the Lord of the Hill; as namely, about what He had done, and wherefore He did what He did, and why He had builded that House. . . . Thus they discoursed together till late at night; and after they had committed themselves to their Lord for protection, they took themselves to rest. The Pilgrim they laid in a large upper chamber, whose window opened towards the Sun rising: the name of the chamber was Peace, where he slept till break of day, and then he awoke and sang,

> Where am I now? Is this the love and care
> Of Jesus, for the men that Pilgrims are
> Thus to provide! That I should be forgiven!
> And dwell already the next door to Heaven!

John Bunyan

L. THAT THEY MAY BE ONE

Why did Jesus command the observation of this rite? He did not give his disciples any other similar instructions about divine worship. Why this? Is it not sufficient to preach and believe his gospel, the gospel of his atoning death? Why this ceremony in our churches? For a long time I asked myself this question . . . without finding the right answer, until the answer sprang to my mind from this text [1 Corinthians 10:16-17]: we must note the dual meaning of the phrase "body of Christ." On the one hand it refers to the body broken for us on the cross at Golgotha: this is symbolized or figuratively expressed in the broken bread, just as the outpoured wine represents the blood of Christ outpoured for us on the cross. That is the usual interpretation which we are familiar with from our confirmation instruction. It is correct in so far as it goes, but it is incomplete. For the body of Christ means in the New Testament something else: the church. The latter is the body of Christ because Christians are incorporated into the eternal Christ by faith and the Holy Ghost. Thus our text says: We who are many are one body. There arises from us who are a multiplicity of individuals, a unity, something whole and cohesive, kneaded together.

Thus what is effected through the common participation in the atoning death of Jesus Christ is the unity of the church. . . . Here is no magic, the bread is not transformed into the body, nor the wine into the blood. But a miracle *does* take place in that those men who formerly were their own lord and master, now are ruled by the one Lord, and so from a manifold of separate individuals, each living and caring for himself, there arises a unity, one body, of which each believer is a member and Jesus Christ the Head, controlling and guiding all. In the eating of the bread and the drinking of the wine, Jesus Christ himself is present to them all and constitutes them as a unity which he controls and directs. They become the body of Jesus Christ.

Emil Brunner

207 *.CHRISTIAN TOGETHERNESS*

The Christian community, the *ekklesia,* is a sacramental community: *communio in sacris,* a "fellowship in holy things," i. e., in the Holy Spirit, or even *communio sanctorum* (*sanctorum* being taken as neuter rather than masculine—perhaps that was the original meaning of the phrase). The unity of the church is effected through the sacraments: baptism and the eucharist are the two "social sacraments" of the church, and in them the true meaning of Christian "togetherness" is continually revealed and sealed. Or even more emphatically, the sacraments constitute the church. Only in the sacraments does the Christian community pass beyond the purely human measure and become the church. . . . Yet sacraments are not merely signs of a professed faith, but rather effective signs of the saving grace—not only symbols of human aspiration and loyalty, but the outward symbols of the divine action. In them our human existence is linked to, or rather raised up to, the divine life, by the Spirit, the giver of life.

Clarence T. Craig

208   *DEMOCRATIC RITE*

When we assemble at the hospitable board of our heavenly Father, we realize our unity as members of his household, and we renew and deepen our fellowship with one another. We meet as brethren who are all one in Christ. Belonging to different families and moving in diverse spheres of society, we recognize at the Lord's table that the spiritual ties which join Christian to Christian are no less real than the ties of blood and friendship. . . . *The holy communion is the most democratic rite that the world has ever known.* It is meant to emancipate Christians from all selfish isolation and narrow individualism, to deliver them from self-valuation and self-interest, and to bring them into a fellowship wide and spacious as the heavens, free and pure as the winds that sweep them, bright as the sun and stars that light them, and bringing a perpetual inspiration to faith and hope, and love for the best and holiest ideals.

J. T. Levens

209   *THE WALLS MELT AWAY*

The observance of World Communion Sunday is the first and as yet the only action in which a considerable share of the 137,000,000 Protestants on earth consciously and simultaneously affirm their unity. They do so in thankful recognition that everywhere, as the earth turns on its axis to bring one land after another to face the sun, Christians lift their eyes to the Son of God in acknowledgment of a fellowship which includes all who take the name of Christ. Because this universal observance is nearest to the inclusive intention of our Lord, this should be the most meaningful communion of the year. On this day the walls of the upper room melt away and we all sit at table with the Master.

World Communion Sunday takes a step in the direction toward which every observance of the Lord's Supper points. Its affirmation of Christian solidarity is certain to strengthen in Protestants a sense of common life, of mutuality, of holy fellowship in the church of Christ. Its wide extension will be rich in the fruits of the Spirit.

Harold E. Fey

210   *THE DEPTH OF LOVE*

We call the Lord's Supper "holy communion" because it is a symbol and a token of the beloved community, the communion of saints. What a wedding ring is to marriage, the holy communion is to the church. It signifies Christian love, the dimension of depth in our relations, the kind of life together in Christ that flows toward the City of God. One day we took communion to one of our church members who was ill in the Veterans Hospital. He said, "My Church hasn't forgotten me." I said, "This communion is a symbol of our prayers for you in Christ's name." It is God's love for us, expressing itself in our love for one another, that creates the church; and in our participation in the church, loving one another in the fellowship of believers, we qualify for eternal life.

Owen Hutchison

211   *THE MASTER'S SOLICITUDE*

His final meeting with his disciples took place in the upper room, on the night of his betrayal. Here Jesus disclosed that his supreme passion and concern was his solicitude for the organic unity of the company of his followers. This was the theme of all his talk and action.

They were eating the Passover. They were twelve men, *plus* One, *plus* God. There had been others. But these others were on the fringe of the fellowship. Jesus . . . saw that he must concentrate upon the twelve, interpreting his public acts and teachings as a physician in his clinic explains his treatment of the patients to the students gathered about him. But all this public work is now past. He is on the point of leaving his disciples. After his departure, disillusionment would seize them. They would surely be tempted to regard all that had happened as a dream. Searching for a word which would steady them in the days ahead, what was it that he most wished them to be aware of?. . . .

He told them something to which he had not called their attention hitherto, because the hour was not ripe. He now focused their attention upon that which had been *happening* to them all along, of which they were unaware, but the understanding of which was now far more important than their understanding of his moral teaching or his messianic mission—more important because it was the primary condition of their ever attaining an understanding of his teaching and his messiahship. You and I, he said, are now bound together in an organic unity. While we have been preaching and teaching and learning, the Father has been working his will in *us;* he has made us one body, a living corporate community. This is the most precious and significant fruit of our association together . . . our communal union—you with one another and with me, and we together with the Father. Our union is inviolable, because it did not arise from your separate individual volitions—it is not your creation, you did not devise it; it "came upon" you as a gift of God. You were "drawn" into it by the Father. You did not choose me, but I chose you; the initiative was mine, not yours; aye, it was not mine, but the Father's whose work I do.

Charles Clayton Morrison

212   *OUT OF TIME INTO ETERNITY*

The greatest thing in the world is a Christian congregation engaged in the supreme act of worship, raised by the fellowship of a noble emotion into the unity of one thought and one love, as we show forth our Lord's death, offering up "a spiritual oblation of all possible praise unto God for the same." Ebenezer Erskine wrote of a night of high experience: "On that night I got my head out of time into eternity." And here we, too, as we watch the shadows gather over Calvary, and see the gloom irradiated by the Lord of Life, triumphant over death, and feel the mystical fellowship of the unnumbered hosts who in all ages have broken the bread and drank of the cup, and see the goal of all our striving shining before us—we, too, get our heads out of time into eternity. For the centuries meet and blend in this act, and the awed heart cannot but say: "Surely the Lord is in this place" (Gen. 28:16).

Norman Maclean

213   *A GLORY FOR ALL MANKIND*

It is not only for the individual that the sacrament of the Lord's Supper has a central, living, mystic meaning, but for the whole community, the whole church, yes, for all mankind. For here the divine mingles with the human, the terrestrial; here in the eucharist praise and sacrifice are offered to the Lord for the whole world and by the whole world. . . . That is why the idea of all creation assembled in spirit round the eucharistic altar so constantly recurs in the old liturgies of the East. For through him, through his death, and through the glorification of his risen body, here mystically represented, creation partakes of the glory of the redemption.

Nicholas Arseniev

214   *A LIVING CENTER OF UNITY*

That supper is an event which profoundly affects the imagination. Its very simplicity increases its significance. The meaning it bears to faith is marvelous on the one hand; the place it has filled, the work it has done in history, as marvelous on the other. If the vision had been granted to Christ to what it was to be and do, would it not, even when his sufferings were deepest, have turned his sorrow into joy? He would have seen his supper surviving for ages, simple in form, transcendent in meaning, a living center of unity for his scattered disciples, a source of comfort, strength, peace, purity to wearied and sinful men. In upper rooms, in catacombs, where the dust of the dead rested, and the spirits of the living met to speak to each other words of holiest cheer; in desert places and moorlands, where hunted fugitives assembled to listen to a voice which, though a man's, seemed God's; in cathedrals, where form and space spoke majestically to the eye, and lofty music to the ear; in rude huts in savage or heathen lands; in ornate churches in wealthy, busy and intellectual cities—men of the most varied types and conditions, saintly and sinful, ignorant and educated, simple and gentle, rich and poor, peer and peasant, sovereign and subject, priest and people, forming a multitude no man can number, have for centuries met together to celebrate this supper, and be by it made wiser, happier, holier.

A. M. Fairbairn

215   *NEED FOR HISTORICAL CONTINUITY*

Nineteen centuries separate us from the upper room, and love, jealous of separation, seeks to find some visible link, some tangible form, by which it may have touch with that remote past. . . .

How thrilling to the imagination is the feast which constitutes a bond, unquestionable and direct, with the upper room itself! Across all the conflict and stress of Asian and African church history, across all the storm-tossed ages of the world, there stretches an unbroken chain, each golden link a eucharist, binding the last communion feast with the first. . . .

When we gather round the Lord's table we look upon, we handle, we taste the elements of bread and wine ordained by Christ. The words of consecration are those which sounded in the ears of the Apostles. The purpose for which we receive it is identical with theirs. The sacrament is the same, and the gift received is the same. The fact is obviously one of the first importance. . . . The holy communion answered exactly to our natural desire for historical continuity. It is of God's goodness that our love, yearning for personal contact, finds its longing met by touch and taste and hearing. . . . In giving to the church this sacrament, Jesus Christ anticipated the needs of love in every age.

Arthur Evelyn Barnes-Lawrence

216   *BOND OF MYSTICAL UNION*

Jesus offered in the church a model of the perfect society, and therefore he established the church on an eternal and universal principle. Wherever a number of isolated individuals come together and form one body there must be some bond of unity. . . . Jesus contemplated a society the most comprehensive and intense, the most elastic and cohesive in history, which would embrace all countries, suit all times, cultivate all varieties, fulfill all aspirations. . . . What is the bond of this mystical union? Jesus stated and vindicated it in the upper room. . . . With St. John and St. Thomas, Matthew the publican and Simon the zealot at the same holy table, it is not likely that Jesus expected one model of thought: with his profound respect for the individual and his sense of the variety of truth, it is certain he did not desire it. Jesus realized that the tie which binds men together in life is not forged in the intellect but in the heart. . . . Love is the first and the last and the strongest bond in experience. It conquers distance, outlives all changes, bears the strain of the most diverse opinions. What a proof of Jesus' divine insight that he . . . did not demand in his farewell that his disciples should think alike, but that they should feel alike. He believed it possible to bind men to their fellows on the one condition that they were first bound fast to him. He made himself the center of eleven men, each an independent unit; he sent through their hearts the electric flash of his love and they became one. It was an experiment on a small scale; it proved a principle that has no limits. Unity is possible whenever the current of love runs from Christ's heart through human hearts and back to Christ again.

John Watson

217   *FELLOWSHIP IN CHRIST*

Here on the table you have the tokens of the broadest and fullest communion. This is a kind of communion which you and I cannot choose or reject: if we are in Christ it is and must be ours. Certain brethren restrict their communion in the outward ordinance, and they think they have good reasons for doing so; but I am unable to see the force of their reasoning, because I joyfully observe that these brethren commune with other believers in prayer, and praise, and hearing of the Word, and other ways, the fact being that the matter of real communion is very largely beyond human control, and is to the spiritual body what the circulation of the blood is to the natural body, a necessary process not dependent upon volition. In pursuing a deeply spiritual book of devotion you have been charmed and benefited, and yet upon looking at the title page it may be you have found that the author belonged to the Church of Rome. What then? Why, then it has happened that the inner life has broken all barriers, and your spirits have communed. . . . Blood is thicker than water, and no fellowship is more inevitable and sincere than fellowship in the precious blood and in the risen life of our Lord Jesus Christ. Here, in the common reception of the one loaf, we bear witness that we are one; and in the actual participation of all the chosen in the one redemption that unity is in very deed displayed and matured in the most substantial manner. Washed in the one blood, fed on the same loaf, cheered by the same cup, all differences pass away, and "we, being many, are one body in Christ, and every one members one of another" (Rom. 12:5).

Charles H. Spurgeon

M. UNTO THE ENDS OF THE EARTH

218   *TO KNEEL WHERE THEY KNELT*

H. R. L. "Dick" Sheppard was once showing a group of visitors through Canterbury Cathedral. When they came to those famous chancel steps, the destination of so many thousands of pilgrim journeys, Sheppard took one man and pressed his knee to the step saying, "Kneel there; it is a great thing to kneel where faithful pilgrims have knelt in days ahead of you."

We do that in the communion of the church. We kneel where others have knelt and then risen to go out victors over the destructive power over alcohol, sex, temper, hate, weakness, fear because they found at the heart of the church One in whose grip they could handle these things. The church is the company of faithful where this power lives. It is a great thing to walk where they walked, kneel where they bowed. You may find this power somewhere outside the church. But it always comes as the overflow *from* the church, a legacy received *through* the church, and unless it leads back *into* the church and joins the body whence it came it shrivels and dies.

Robert E. Luccock

219   *SUNDAY WORSHIP IN ROME (ca. 140 A.D.)*

On finishing the prayers we greet each other with a kiss. Then bread and a cup of water and mixed wine are brought to the president of the brethren and he, taking them, sends up praise and glory to the Father of the universe through the name of the Son and of the Holy Spirit, and offers thanksgiving at some length that we have been deemed worthy to receive these things from him. When he has finished the prayers and the thanksgiving, the whole congregation present assents, saying, "Amen." "Amen" in the Hebrew language means, "So be it." When the president has given thanks and the whole congregation has assented, those whom we call deacons give to each of those present a portion of the consecrated bread and wine and water, and they take it to the absent.

This food we call eucharist, of which no one is allowed to partake except one who believes that the things we teach are true, and has received the washing for forgiveness of sins and for rebirth, and who lives as Christ handed down to us. For we do not receive these things as common bread or common drink. . . .

Those who prosper, and so wish, contribute, each one as much as he chooses to. What is collected is deposited with the president, and he takes care of orphans and widows, and those who are in want on account of sickness or any other cause, and those who are in bonds, and the strangers who are sojourners among [us], and, briefly, he is the protector of all those in need.

We all hold this common gathering on Sunday, since it is the first day, on which God transforming darkness and matter made the universe, and Jesus Christ our Saviour rose from the dead on the same day.

Justin Martyr

220   POLYCARP KEEPS THE FAITH

Every time that we take part in the eucharist, we are ourselves another link in the chain of uninterrupted celebration of the sacrament, which has never ceased, from the Last Supper down to the present moment. We are in a glorious succession. Think of Polycarp, Bishop of Smyrna, who had learned much of Christ from John, the disciple of the Lord, at Ephesus, and was an intimate friend of "those who had seen the Lord." Born about the year 70 (or possibly a little earlier) Polycarp, as a young man, must have often worshipped at the eucharist when John was officiating. How moving it must have been for him to hear the words: "This do in remembrance of me," pronounced by one who had known the Lord on earth. It was in this faith and love that Polycarp lived and prayed and served Christ, and in this faith he died. He was a very old man when persecution broke out at Smyrna. Yet when he was brought before the authorities and urged to sacrifice to Caesar, and thus to save his life, he had only one thing to say: "Eighty and six years have I served Christ, and he never did me wrong; how can I now blaspheme my King that has saved me?" When he was bound to the stake and about to be burned, he prayed: "I bless thee that thou hast thought me worthy of the present day and hour, to have a share in the number of martyrs, and in the cup of Christ, unto the resurrection of eternal life."

Polycarp had kept the "feast of redemption" all through his long and blameless life. He had "remembered" Christ in the sacrament, but it was no mere "memory" but his living Presence that strengthened him for service and endurance to the very end. Polycarp drank the "cup of Christ" when he gave his body to be burned rather than deny his Lord.

Olive Wyon

221 COMMUNION AT JAMESTOWN

When I went first to Virginia, I well remember wee did hang an awning (which is an old saile) to three or foure trees to shadow us from the sunne, our walles were rales of wood, our seats unhewed trees till we cut plankes, our pulpit a bar of wood nailed to two neighbouring trees. In foule weather we shifted into an old rotten tent; for we had few better, and this came by the way of adventure for new. This was our church, till wee built a homely thing like a barne, set upon cratchets, covered with rafts, sedge, and earth; so was also the walls: the best of our houses [were] of like curiosity; but the most part farre much worse workmanship, that could neither well defend [from] wind nor raine. Yet wee had daily common prayer morning and evening, every Sunday two sermons, and every three moneths the holy communion. . . . And surely God did most mercifully heare us.

John Smith

222 WASHINGTON AT COMMUNION

When the American army, under the command of Washington, lay encamped in the environs of Morristown, New Jersey, it occurred that the service of the communion (there observed semi-annually only) was to be administered in the Presbyterian Church of that village. On a morning of a previous week, the general after his accustomed inspection of the camp, visited the house of the Rev. Doctor Jones, the pastor of the church, and after the usual preliminaries, thus accosted him: "Doctor, I understand that the Lord's Supper is to be celebrated with you next Sunday; I would learn if it accords with the canons of your church to admit communicants of another denomination?" The doctor rejoined: "Most certainly; ours is not the Presbyterian table, General, but the Lord's table; and we hence give the Lord's invitation to all his followers of whatever name." The general replied: "I am glad of it; that is as it ought to be; but as I was not quite sure of the fact, I thought I would ascertain it from yourself, as I propose to join with you on that occasion. Though a member of the Church of England, I have no exclusive partialities." The doctor assured him of a cordial welcome, and the general was found seated with the communicants the next Lord's Day.

The Christian-Evangelist

223   WILLIAM CAREY'S FIRST CONVERT

On Monday, December 22 [1800], [John] Thomas asked Krishna whether he understood what he had learned. He replied that "the Lord Jesus Christ had given his very life for the salvation of sinners and that he and his friend Gokul did unfeignedly believe this."

"Then you are our brothers," said Thomas. "Come, and in love let us eat together.". . . . Gokul and Krishna consenting, they sat down with the mission families and ate with them, having first withdrawn into a quiet place for prayer.

A eucharist indeed! The Master was once more made known to me in the breaking of bread. . . .

Hell's wolves compassed and bayed round Krishna's home. At dawn they haled him before a magistrate, who sent them to the governor. "This man," they shouted, "has eaten with Europeans, and has become one."

"Nay," answered the valiant old governor, as soon as he learned the facts, "he has become a Christian, not European, and he has done well. I will answer all demands against him. I forbid you to harm him."

They withdrew from the governor's presence, but could not be quieted. Some had already snatched from Krishna his eldest daughter, as contracted months before for marriage to a Hindu neighbor. Hundreds mobbed and mocked him. . . .

Carey met Rasamayi [Krishna's wife], frightened and sobbing in the road, and wept with her. . . . "Fidelity to Christ has brought you this trouble. He'll treasure your tears . . . and will never forsake you."

They would all, however, have been murdered that night had not the governor learned of the plot, and sent a guard to protect them. Then kinsfolk and neighbors plied all pleas, taunts, threats to break their baptismal purpose. . . . [Krishna] only smiled and gave the reason for his confidence.

Of the historic baptism [Carey's first in fifteen years of missionary endeavor in India], [William] Ward [an associate of Carey] wrote: "After our English Service . . . we went to the riverside. . . . We sang in Bengali, 'Jesus, and shall it ever be?'. . . . After prayer [Carey] went down the bank into the water. . . . Then Krishna went down and was baptized, the words in Bengali. . . . Almost every one seemed struck with the solemnity of this new ordinance. I never saw in the most orderly congregation in England anything more impressive. . . . In the afternoon we kept the Lord's Supper in Bengali for the first time. . . . About nine o'clock Krishna came joyfully to the mission to tell us that [his relatives from Chandernagore and Calcutta] wished for baptism."

S. Pearce Carey

224 *FIRST COMMUNION*

Our first communion on Aniwa . . . was Sabbath, 24th October, 1869; and surely the angels of God and the Church of the Redeemed in Glory were amongst the great cloud of witnesses who eagerly "peered" down upon the scene—when we sat around the Lord's Table and partook of his body and blood with those few souls rescued out of the heathen world. . . . On that Lord's Day, after the usual opening service, I gave a short and careful exposition of the Ten Commandments and of the way of salvation according to the Gospel. . . .

Beginning with the old Chief, the twelve [candidates] came forward, and I baptized them one by one. . . . Solemn prayer was then offered, and in the name of the Holy Trinity the Church of Christ on Aniwa was formally constituted. I addressed them on the words of the holy institution—I Corinthians xi. 23—and then, after the prayer of thanksgiving and consecration, administered the Lord's Supper—the first time since the Island of Aniwa was heaved out of its coral depths! . . . I think, if ever in all my earthly experience, on that day I might truly add the blessed words—Jesus "in the midst."

The whole service occupied nearly three hours. The Islanders looked on with a wonder whose unwonted silence was almost painful to hear. . . . For three years we had toiled and prayed and taught for this. At the moment when I put the bread and wine into those dark hands, once stained with the blood of cannibalism, now stretched out to receive and partake the emblems and seals of the Redeemer's love, I had a foretaste of the joy of Glory that well nigh broke my heart to pieces. I shall never taste a deeper bliss, till I gaze on the glorified face of Jesus himself.

John G. Paton

225 *"FATHER, FORGIVE THEM"*

In New Zealand the Lord's Supper was being celebrated. The first rank having knelt, a native rose up and returned to his seat, but again returned to the rank and knelt down. Being questioned, he said, "When I went to the table I did not know whom I should have to kneel beside, when suddenly I saw by my side the man who a few years before slew my father and drank his blood, and whom I then devoted to death. Imagine what I felt when I suddenly found him by my side. A rush of feeling came over me that I could not endure, and I went back to my seat. But when I got there, I saw the Upper Sanctuary and the Great Supper and I thought I heard a voice saying, 'By this shall all men know that ye are my disciples if ye love one another.' That overpowered me. I sat down, and at once seemed to see another vision of a cross with a Man nailed to it; and I heard him say, 'Father, forgive them, for they know not what they do.' Then I returned to the altar."

P. J. Maclagen

226   *IN THE PRESENCE OF THEIR ENEMIES*

In the First World War Karl Barth was present at a Roman Catholic service somewhere in the war area. During the celebration of the mass a shell crashed into the building and burst. The priest waited till the dust cleared and the debris subsided, then quietly proceeded with the service, as if nothing had happened. Apparently something much more important was being done in this service than was covered by the effects of enemy action. . . . . The history of Covenanting Scotland bears eloquent tribute to the power of witness that lies in public worship. When men hold conventicles in the open air, with human bloodhounds baying at their feet, and when they spread the Lord's Table literally in the presence of their enemies, they are most certainly publicizing their sense of the worth of these things.

Robert Menzies

227   *BATTLE SCENE*

Last Tuesday I had my first communion service out here in France. We could not get a room of any kind, so we held the service in the corner of a field behind some billets. I spread my mackintosh on the grass and it served for a table; I used the communion service which was given me when I left the old country. Twelve men formed a semi-circle round me, and the evening shadows were gathering over us when I began to read the words, "Dearly beloved in the Lord." Then in the twilight the twelve came one by one and knelt upon the corner of the mackintosh and received the broken bread and outpoured wine. As we knelt together in holy communion we could hear the voices of men returning from a game of football in a neighboring field. As they passed through an opening in the hedge near us, they lowered their voices and passed quietly on to their billets in the village. When each of the twelve soldiers had partaken, and returned to his place, I gave out, verse by verse, by the help of an electric torch, "When I survey the wondrous cross." In the utter stillness of the fields we sang, and, although between the verses we could hear the low booming of the distant guns, we rejoiced in the love of God revealed in Christ Jesus.

Thomas Tiplady

228 FROM MANY, ONE

A Dutch cabinet minister, two Norwegian shippers, a British major from the Indian army, a Yugoslavian diplomat, and a Macedonian journalist constituted the small congregation for which, for the first time after seven and a half years, I conducted a religious service. It was on Christmas Eve in 1944, during post arrest in the Dachau concentration camp. Since all six members of the congregation spoke tolerably good German, their understanding did not present great difficulties. Indeed, we sang our German chorals with a zest and joy to be found in few congregations of our homeland. Our congregation, moreover, was almost as rich in denominations as in nationalities: Calvinists, Lutherans, Anglicans, and Greek Orthodox found themselves together here—nearly all isolated individuals who were cut off and separated from their religious communities as much as from their families and friends. What else was left to us than to put into practice now, as well as we understood it, the *una sancta,* the one Holy Church, and to gather together around God's word? Nay, what else was left to us than also to celebrate our Lord's Supper? Indeed we did it, and all of us rejoiced with all our hearts in the communion that united us as disciples of the same Teacher and Savior.

Martin Niemöller

229 FORETASTE OF THE FUTURE

At the Amsterdam Assembly, Dr. Edmund Schlink of the University of Heidelberg described in these words the meaning of the Lord's Supper to German Christians during the Nazi rule: "People gathered afresh around the sacraments. The number of communion services and of communicants increased. In the midst of this tribulation and distress there awakened a new longing for the concrete, personal experience of receiving the body and blood of the incarnate Son of God who has given himself for us. This destroyed the oppressive solemnity of the memorial services, the form in which the communion services had largely been celebrated. By receiving the body which Jesus Christ gave for us on the cross, we realized that this same Christ gives himself to us in the sacrament as the Risen Lord, who will come again. In the sacrament, through sharing in Jesus' death on Golgotha, we realized more and more that, in this same sacrament, we also share in the great sacrament to which he will call his own from all over the world, to celebrate it with them in God's Kingdom. But looking forward to his return, we already received the foretaste of the future marriage feast which the Lamb will celebrate with his bride, the church, at the end of time, for ever and ever. These communion services echoed the joy of the early Christians, to whom the body and blood of Christ were objects of the greatest joy and praise."

230   *HOUSEHOLD OF FAITH*

The eucharist is likewise a family meal. As such, it has among Christians the place which the Passover filled in the religious experience of the ancient Hebrews. The Passover was pre-eminently a family meal. While those people were to give thanks to God for their deliverance as a nation, in the service itself the unit was the family. This seems to have been one of God's ways of teaching those childlike people that the most important place on earth is the home, and that worship ought to be at its best in the family circle. In the New Testament, also, there is much emphasis on the home as the center of life on earth, and on religion as centering in the family, rather than the individual or the nation. The celebration of the sacrament in the days of the Apostles seems to have been that of one large household coming together to rejoice in God and in each other.

It should still be possible for us to preserve the idea of communing as families, even when we all come together in the House of the Lord. In the olden days, the Scotch custom was to celebrate the sacrament at a long table, spread with linen spotless white. At each end of the table would stand one of the elders to receive from every communicant a little brass token as a visible symbol of his being a member of the church. At the proper time the members of the congregation would come forward by families. First would be the father, then the mother, and after them the sons and daughters, according to their years.

Andrew W. Blackwood

N. MARRIAGE SUPPER OF THE LAMB

231   *FESTIVAL OF HOPE*

The holy communion is a festival of hope. It carries us forward in faith and expectation to the heavenly feast which it foreshadows. When they gathered in the upper room, the twelve were on the eve of a heavy bereavement. The Master whom they loved and to whom they had clung like children to their father, would presently be taken from them, and they must face the world's contempt and hostility without his guidance and comfort. But he told them that their separation was only for a season. They would meet him again in the Father's house and sit with him at a nobler and gladder feast.

And this consolation is offered to us even as to them. Is the holy table ever spread but some one takes his place among the guests with a cruel sorrow in his heart? There is a vacant place by his side. The voice is silent that used to blend with his in the psalm of thanksgiving. . . . It seems as though the house of communion must be evermore for him a place of sad regret. Nay, it is his place of comfort. For what is the message from the holy supper? "Courage!" it says: "Bethink you of the heavenly feast whereof this table is a dim foreshadowing. Lift up your heart to the City of God and the Father's house. Your dead is there, and you will meet again in blessed reunion. You will look again upon each other's faces, and clasp each other's hands, and sit together in holier fellowship at a gladder feast."

David Smith

232   *JOYOUS ANTICIPATION*

And he said to them, "This is my blood of the covenant, which is poured out for many. Truly, I say to you, I shall not drink again of the fruit of the vine until that day when I drink it new in the kingdom of God."

MARK 14:24-25, RSV

Even at the end, there is a note of anticipation in the song of farewell. "Until I drink it new"—this is both denouement and anticipation. Jesus looks forward to that time of the future consummation of the Kingdom, when the "Bridegroom" has come, and he can sit down with those of his fellowship and covenant and break bread in the Kingdom of God that knows no end. The Lord's Supper then should not only be a Supper of remembrance, but a Supper of joyous anticipation. We look forward as well as backward at the table of our Lord.

Ernest Lee Stoffel

233   THEIR SHARE IN THE GLORY

In giving his disciples the broken bread and the cup, our Lord was initiating them into "the sufferings of Christ, and the glory [to] follow" (1 Pet. 1:11). They were thereby united with him in the life laid down and raised in glory. The sacrament is indeed for them still proleptic or anticipatory, for though he celebrates it in the presence of his finished work, that work is not in fact finished. His act, like the symbolic acts of the prophets, not merely declares, but helps to bring about that which God has willed. It is a *signum efficax*. The situation brings out very clearly the truth that this participation of the disciples in the life of the Kingdom of God is wholly of grace and not of merit. They are so little worthy of it that they will deny or forsake their Lord. Yet he gives them bread and cup, sealing them for that which is to come. The subsequent experience of the disciples, to which the whole New Testament bears witness, affords proof that his gift was in fact efficacious.

C. H. Dodd

234   ORIENTATION TOWARDS THE FUTURE

Jesus gave to the Last Supper, and hence to the sacrament, a decisive eschatological orientation when he said, "Verily I say unto you, I will drink no more of the fruit of the vine, until that day that I drink it new [with you, Matthew justly interprets] in the kingdom of God" (Mark 14:25). The wine, we are to understand, is to partake of the newness of the new heavens and the new earth which will be revealed in the Day of the Lord. Here Jesus is not viewing this great day on the side which is now turned towards us—this side which threatens judgment and prompts us to repentance—but on the bright side which will not be visible to us till after the regeneration. His decisive orientation towards the future may explain why Jesus did not speak of the sacrament as a retrospective memorial of him, although it was sure to acquire this significance eventually. Paul emphasizes the memorial character of the sacrament when he says, "Ye do shew the Lord's death till he come" (1 Cor. 11:26). But the second coming is prospective, and even the proclamation of the

Lord's death is not wholly retrospective, being an instance of the proclamation of the gospel, which always has in view a future salvation. This is the sense in which the bread and the wine—Jesus' body and blood—are given and taken and eaten in remembrance of him.

Walter Lowrie

235   *THE PROMISE OF HIS COMING*

Nor let us suppose that by once or twice seeking God in this gracious ordinance, we can secure the gift forever: "Seek the Lord and his strength, seek his face continually" (1 Chron. 16:11). The bread which comes down from heaven is like the manna, "daily bread," and that "till he come," till his "kingdom come." In his coming at the end of the world, all our wishes and prayers rest and are accomplished; and in his present communion we have a stay and consolation meanwhile, joining together the past and future, reminding us that he has come once, and promising that he will come again. . . . While the times wax old, and the colors of earth fade, and the voice of song is brought low, and all kindreds of the earth can but wail and lament, the sons of God lift up their heads, for their salvation draweth nigh. Nature fails, the sun shines not, and the moon is dim, the stars fall from heaven, and the foundations of the round world shake; but the altar's light burns ever brighter; there are sights there which the many cannot see, and all above the tumults of earth the command is heard to show forth the Lord's death, and the promise that the Lord is coming.

John Henry Newman

O. SACRAMENT OF TOWEL
AND BASIN

236   *HE TOOK A SLAVE'S PLACE*

I once asked a group of Chinese pastors in an interior town what it was in Christ that most impressed them. None of them mentioned the account of any miracle. Chinese mythology could outdo the marvels recorded on Gospel pages. Various replies were given, when one elderly man said: "His washing his disciples' feet," and a sudden general consensus showed that this incident was peculiarly appealing to them. That a revered Teacher should overstep the lines of class and position and take a slave's place was an impressive moral miracle.

Henry Sloane Coffin

237   *REMEMBERING WHO HE WAS*

Jesus knowing . . . that he was come from God, and went to God . . . began to wash the disciples' feet.   JOHN 13:3, 5.

Jesus, remembering who he was, remembering his rank, his dignity, his name, stooped to do the lowliest service. . . . Think how differently it affects many, and is apt to affect us all, to recall any circumstance about ourselves, our birth, our education, our place in the world. . . . How often is it not the case that the very thing which led Jesus to this lowly service has the very contrary effect upon us. . . . Remembering who he was, he rose and washed the disciples' feet. Remembering who we are, we are tempted in various ways to gather our robes about us and pass on.

John A. Hutton

238   *A NEW ORDER OF GREATNESS*

One wonders what emotions surged in the heart of Jesus as he came to Judas in that dramatized teaching, "The Sacrament of the Towel and Basin." Is there anything to be done for a failure of a man, a traitor who has already sold out to the enemy? Perhaps there was a moment of hestitation. What deep expression of pain and perplexity must have settled on his face! Should he cast pearls before swine? It is obvious that a dictator would show no mercy toward a traitor in the inner circle. But Jesus was not a dictator, he was the Suffering Servant who staked his Kingdom on deeds of helpfulness and whose love overleaped the boundaries of misunderstanding and prejudice. So he bends to the task. The water splashes in the basin for Judas and the next moment he is looking down upon the bowed head of the Master—the most eloquent plea a man ever made for the recovery of a man who had gone wrong in the head and heart. Yea, more, it was the introduction of Judas and the world to a new order of greatness.

Frederick Keller Stamm

239 *HIS SPIRIT OF LOWLY SERVICE*

One very arresting peculiarity of St. John's Gospel is that the writer entirely ignores the institution of the Lord's Supper. . . . The reason seems to be that by St. John's day, the sacrament had come to be sadly misused. The simple means of grace that our Lord bequeathed had become more than tainted with magical ideas. Too many people were taking it for granted that the bread and wine, of themselves, had saving power. . . . To St. John with his passion for the spiritual significance of everything in the Gospel-story all that ascribing of redemptive virtue to the mere elements was anathema and made a travesty of the sacrament.

His silence as to the institution is deliberate and pointed and what he substitutes here is his quiet way of saying: "Precious as the outward sign may be—it was of our Lord's own choosing—vital beyond measure is the thing signified. Of what avail are the bread and wine if they do not cry to your soul of the Lord's atoning death? Of what use are they if, in receiving them, you do not receive his own spirit of lowly service and self-consecration? The spirit of his you will see shining in its splendor here, where Jesus kneels and washes the feet of his disciples."

Adam W. Burnet

240 *CONDITIONS FOR DISCIPLESHIP*

In St. John's Gospel there is no narrative of the institution of the eucharist. Instead, we are given (John 13-17) first the acted parable of the foot washing, to teach us the lesson of humility which no one needs more than the "regular communicant." And then, in the great discourses in the upper room, we are shown the meaning both of communion and of sacrifice. The disciples of Christ are like the branches of the vine which draw all their life from the stem: severed from it, they die. "Without me ye can do nothing" (John 15:5). The life of the vine is the sap which springs from the root to course through every branch and tendril; and that is Christ's own love for his disciples, in which he calls them to abide—the love of which St. Paul speaks as a constraining, unifying power. At one point the allegory seems to break down. The disciples are told that there is a condition which must be fulfilled if they are to abide in his love, to be healthy branches of the vine. That condition is that they keep his new commandment, which is that they love one another. They cannot receive and be vivified by the love which is Christ's gift of himself to his whole church, except by truly sharing it: they must be ready to lay down their lives for their friends. For the branches of the vine do not exist for their own sakes: it is not enough for them to be so many parts of a growing plant. The vine fulfils its creative purpose in the fruit which its branches bear; and as every gardener knows, the shoots which are allowed to absorb the sap only to enlarge themselves will not be fruitful. There the allegory is left. We are told no more of the fruit than that it serves the glory of God. But we cannot mistake the reference to the pruning knife; and it is hardly fanciful to link the fruit of the vine with the cup of the Last Supper and its symbolism of sacrifice.

John Burnaby

P. THE HAND OF THE BETRAYER

241   *COUNTERFEITED GOODNESS*

Judas, betrayest thou the Son of man with a kiss?   LUKE 22:48

To use a kiss in the ministry of betrayal is like using a sacramental cup to poison a friend. The very worst form of devilry is that which garbs itself in the robes of an angel of light. Evil which wears its own clothes is sufficiently repulsive, but it is not nearly so repulsive as when it counterfeits goodness, and decks itself in adornments stolen from the wardrobe of virtue. If betrayal comes with a curse and a frown we know how to interpret its approach, but when it comes with smiles and kisses it can deceive the very elect. This kiss of Judas wounded the Lord far more deeply than did the nails which fastened him to the cross.

John Henry Jowett

242   *TO SERVE OR TO BETRAY*

There came unto him a woman having an alabaster box of very precious ointment, and poured it on his head, as he sat at meat. . . . Then Judas, which betrayed him, answered and said, Master, is it I? He said unto him, Thou hast said.   MATTHEW 26:7, 25

These are two pictures: one of devotion and the other of denial, one of generosity and the other of apostasy, one of light and the other of darkness, one the face of a saint and the other the face of a traitor, one with the morning light and the other in the gloom of midnight. But each picture has the same lesson.

Both are saying that the main thing is our attitude to Christ. We cannot ignore him. We must be one thing or another, friend or foe, and that which shapes life is not so much our feeling about humanity, or even our attitude to the church. The holiest act of life is to serve him; the basest, to betray him.

Coming to the communion table, this is the question for the heart to answer: What have I for Christ? Can I bring him some alabaster box of very precious ointment, or am I ready to betray him? Christ is still betrayed, and sometimes for less than thirty pieces of silver, sometimes for a passing hour of pleasure, sometimes for the smile of a Christless world. Sometimes we betray him at the very table where he calls us to remember him.

James I. Vance

243   *THE OUTPOURED LOVE*

The question often debated—whether Judas ate of the broken bread at the Last Supper—is . . . answered by the Fourth Evangelist. Yet! he would say, he did indeed eat it, for to him it was especially offered. Jesus gave to Judas the piece of bread dipped in the wine. The two symbols of the outpoured love were received by him. The offering of the morsel to Judas was the Evangelist's symbolical way of speaking of the offering of the love of Jesus to Judas which he spurned. As the broken bread symbolized the life given on the cross, so the sop offered to Judas is symbolical of that same self-giving in love. The Evangelist does not narrate "the breaking of the bread"; but in relating the offering of the morsel dipped in wine to Judas he says all that the former had said— *and more.* And the *one thing more* which this latter act said, was that the self-giving of Jesus was not only for such disciples as had responded to his love, but was also for Judas—and such as Judas—who bitterly spurned that love.

C. J. Wright

244   *ALL ARE TRAITORS*

The same night in which he was betrayed.
1 CORINTHIANS 11:23

What crime has more likeness to the night than a betrayal? And what crime is more unlike love than a betrayal? Most of all, alas, when it is accomplished with a kiss! Judas indeed is the traitor, but at bottom all are traitors, only not like him for money. Judas betrays him to the high priests, and the high priests betray him to the people, and the people betray him to Pilate, and Pilate for fear of the emperor betrays him to death, and for fear of man those disciples do the same who flee in the night, and Peter who denies him in the court. This was the last betrayal. Oh, when the last spark is extinguished, how dark it all is! Of the whole race there is not one, not a single man, who will have anything to do with him—and *he is the truth!* And, oh, if thou art inclined to think that thou wouldst never have done this, never have laid thy hand upon him, never have taken part in the mockery—but as for betraying him, that thou hast done: thou didst flee, or didst shrewdly remain at home, keeping thyself out of it, letting thy servant report to thee what happened. Oh, but to betray! Thou canst deal love no blow so painful! There is no pain, not even the most torturing bodily pain, at which love winces so feelingly as betrayal; for the greatest felicity of love is faithfulness.

Søren Kierkegaard

245   *IS IT I, LORD?*

Already he had made arrangements to betray Jesus by promising to lead the temple soldiers to his secret place of prayer. Even so, Jesus would not give up in his attempt to win Judas. He decided to tell them all as they sat about the table that one of them would betray him. They were shocked, stunned into silence, and then they burst into questions, "Is it I, Lord?" (Matt. 26:22). Jesus hoped that Judas would feel the enormity of his deed as the disciples reacted to his statement, that he would see himself and his act in their true light. Matthew indicates, however, that even Judas joined in the questioning: "Is it I, Master?" he said. He was carrying out his intention with a gesture of innocency. The Gospel of John states, in addition, that Jesus pointed out the betrayer by dipping a morsel of bread into his own cup and handing it to Judas. This was, in reality, an expression of love toward Judas for the giving of the sop was intended customarily for the honored guest. Judas accepted it without a murmur of protest, giving the appearance of good faith. At this point John states with great insight, "Then after the morsel, Satan entered into him" (John 13:27, RSV). The light of his soul had gone out. He continued in his determination to sin against love.

Charles M. Laymon

246   *A SEARCHING OF SOULS*

We call the disciples saints now, but the night they sat together at the Last Supper they were not saints by any possible stretch of the imagination. They had quarreled over the chief seats in the Kingdom of God. They had wanted to destroy an unfriendly Samaritan village. Shortly, they were to desert their Master. One of them would betray him, another deny him, and in the stress of the Garden of Gethsemane "they all forsook him and fled" (Mark 14:50).

Nevertheless, Jesus believed in the twelve. Quite possibly he trusted in the mood in them which revealed itself at the Last Supper when he calmly announced: "One of you will betray me" (Mark 14:18). He noted that not one of the twelve looked at another of the company to ask, "Is it he?" On the contrary, there was a searching of souls and a single question from the lips of each of those who sat with Jesus: "Master, is it I?" The sainthood of the twelve began with that question, for it reflected an honest awareness of the menace in each one. They still were self-possessed and still would seek to save themselves when crisis came. They knew in their own minds that any one of them was capable of betrayal.

Harold Blake Walker

247   *WHERE CONFLICTS CEASE*

Bassano, whose painting of the Last Supper hangs in the Madrid Museum, pictures Judas with his back to the spectator, while in the angle of the supper table a dog and cat are quarreling over a bone. Other artists bring out the same idea of quarreling. There was discord there, but Jesus was never guilty of quarreling with his disciples. They quarreled with each other. It is interesting to note that Judas has his back to the spectator. Can we blame Judas for having such a desire as was depicted by Bassano? There was a lack of harmony there. Then I only ask—what better place is afforded the modern Christian to settle disputes with the Lord, with his neighbor, with his church, than at communion altars? Friction vanishes at that place of prayer! Devotees of Christ have arisen from such altars to go and make necessary restitution. They knelt in weakness. They arose with clean hearts, and purposes strengthened by the Spirit.

Edward Jeffries Rees

Q. AND THEY SANG A HYMN

248 *ANTHEM OF EMANCIPATION*

When they had sung a hymn, they went out unto the mount of Olives.
MATTHEW 26:30

These words, interpreted by a reverent imagination, present one of the most wonderful pictures. Twelve men are seen singing together. The company is composed of One, and eleven. The circumstances, judged by human standards, can only be described as tragic. The eleven are losing the One. He is going out to bruising, to buffeting, to a death of shame. And yet they sing, and it is impossible to doubt that he led the singing. We shall be helped in considering the wonder if we glance at Psalms 113 to 118. These constituted the Great Hallel which was always sung at the Passover.

All that had been foreshadowed in that feast was now approaching completion, and this company of eleven were permitted to join him, the Paschal Lamb by God appointed, in singing.

If we are amazed at a song in so dark an hour, we also see its fitness and its glory. If they thought they were losing him, it was not so in the counsel of God. He was gaining them, that so they might gain him, in a sense in which they had never possessed him. He was going forth to bruise the head of the serpent, to put to shame all the evil things that had destroyed men. He was passing in travail to the final triumph. No sweeter singing, no mightier music ever sounded amid the darkness of the sad world's night than the singing of Jesus and his first disciples, as he moved out to the cross of his passion, and their redemption. They sang the anthem of humanity's emancipation and of God's glory. And so persistently, through all the ages, those who have fellowship with his suffering march along the sorrowful way, singing the song of final triumph.

G. Campbell Morgan

249 *THEY SANG A HYMN*

And when they had sung an hymn, they went out into the mount of Olives. MATTHEW 26:30

In some respects this is one of the most remarkable statements in the life of our Savior. We have seen him in various conditions and circumstances . . . but never before in the exercise of vocal praise. . . . We have sat with him at his sacramental table, and listened to those simple, touching and profound discourses, which he spake in that hour of wistful expectation. But now the little assembly is broken up. . . . They descend from that upper chamber, and as the shadows of evening gather about them, bend their steps to the eastern ravine, through which the Kedron pours its scanty rill, and upward on the first ascending slope of the Mount of Olives. There, a little above the lowest part, was the Garden of Gethsemane, affording among its olive shades a retirement suited for meditation and prayer, to which Jesus had often been accustomed to resort. But the ascent hither is not silent. The voice of harmony breaks upon the stillness of this memorable night. They sang a hymn. It is not unlikely that they sang it as they walked. . . . Who knows but that the hymn which they sang was one in which they had joined again and again with their Lord and Master? It is presumed that they all sang. . . . Which of the eleven would willingly have been dumb at such a moment, if only he comprehended the significance of the hour? . . . Could we fully reproduce the strain, we should find in it probably nothing that meets the requisition of artistic taste. But it was assuredly elevated by the high solemnity of the scene, and broken into tremulous notes by the gush of pensive emotion.

James W. Alexander

250   *WHAT THE HYMN MEANT TO JESUS*

Probably Jesus alone knew what the singing of this hymn meant—that it was the last hymn they would sing together, the last hymn he would sing on earth; and from that point of view it would be a great experience for him, helping him, we have no doubt, to bear what he had to pass through that night and next day. He would like to feel that he stood in the tradition of his fathers, that he was singing, as a full-grown man understanding why, what he had sung as a prattling child by his mother's side. He would feel, too, that what he was about to do—to lay down his life in love—was no strange thing really; that it was what the best souls of his own beloved people had done in all the ages that were past, though in his own case it was something more than a repetition of their faithfulness.

John A. Hutton

251   *OUR SINGING-MASTER*

Let us dwell a while on the fact that Jesus sang at such a time as this. What does he teach us by it? Does he not say to each of us, his followers: "My religion is one of happiness and joy; I, your Master, by my example would instruct you to sing even when the last solemn hour is come and all the glooms of death are gathering around you. Here, at the table, I am your singing-master, and set you lessons in music, in which my dying voice shall lead you: notwithstanding all the griefs which overwhelm my heart, I will be to you the chief musician and the sweet singer of Israel." If ever there was a time when it would have been natural and consistent with the solemnities of the occasion for the Savior to have bowed his head upon the table, bursting into a flood of tears; or, if ever there was a season when he might have fittingly returned from all company, and have bewailed his coming conflict in sighs and groans, it was just then. But no, that brave heart will sing "an hymn." Our glorious Jesus plays the man beyond all other men. Boldest of the sons of men, he quails not in the hour of battle, but tunes his voice to loftiest psalmody. The genius of Christianity of which Jesus is the head and founder, its object, spirit, and design, are happiness and joy, and they who receive it are able to sing in the very jaws of death.

Charles H. Spurgeon

252   *THE WORDS OF THEIR SONG*

The saying of Grace after meat was followed immediately by the singing of the Hymn of Praise, Psalms 114-118 (Mark 14:26 par.). It was antiphonal: one member of the table fellowship recited the text, and the others responded to each half-verse with "Hallelujah." Jesus' great knowledge of the Bible warrants the assumption that he himself sang the *Hallēl*. However that may be, whether he recited it or whether he only joined in the prayer and the responses, we know the prayers with which Jesus concluded the Last Supper. They are all prayers of thanksgiving. They praise the Deliverer from the power of the Egyptians, before whose presence the earth trembles (Ps. 114). They praise him as the one, the only living God in whom his chosen people put their trust, who blesses those who fear him, and who will be blessed for evermore (Ps. 115). They promise to the merciful Redeemer who has delivered their soul from death, sacrifices of thanksgiving and the payment of vows in the presence of all his people (Ps. 116). They call upon the heathen to join in praise (Ps. 117). And they close with a prayer expressing the thanksgiving and the jubilation of the festal community: "O give thanks unto the Lord; for he is good: because his mercy endureth for ever" (Ps. 118:1). Out of my distress the Lord has heard me. Now the songs of jubilation resound: "I shall not die, but live, and declare the words of the Lord" (v. 17); the rejected stone has become the keystone through God's action (vv. 22-23); "blessed be he that cometh in the name of the Lord" (v. 26); "thou art my God, I will exalt thee; O give thanks unto the Lord; for he is good: for his mercy endureth for ever" (vv. 28-29). Jesus prayed in these very words.

We know that especially the last verses of the *Hallēl* had been much in Jesus' mind: the Hosanna (Ps. 118:25-26), the jubilant shout of the people going in procession round the altar with palms in their hands at the Feast of the Tabernacles, was sung to him by the crowd at his entry into Jerusalem (Mark 11:9-10); in the saying about the rejected stone which God has made the keystone (Ps. 118:22) he saw a prophecy of his death and subsequent exaltation (Mark 8:31; cf., 12:10-11; Luke 17:25); he described the exclamation "blessed be he that cometh in the name of the Lord" (Ps. 118:26) as the salutation with which Israel, that now rejects him, will greet him as king (Matt. 23:39 par.). Like many contemporary commentators, Jesus also gave an eschatological-Messianic meaning to Psalm 118, and applied it to himself: he found in this psalm a description of how God would guide his Messiah through suffering to glory and of the ceaseless divine praises of the ages to come. When he arose to go to Gethsemane, this psalm was on his lips.

Joachim Jeremias

R. TESTIMONY OF THE REFORMATION

THE NORM OF WORSHIP

The Reformation was grounded first of all in the belief that the eucharist, the Lord's Supper, was the norm of worship if not the normal weekly service of the Christian community. . . .

Luther, Calvin, the Anglican Reformation, the early English Baptists and Congregationalists, the Methodists, and the Disciples of Christ, despite their different nuances and varying testimonies, are all rooted in a liturgical movement. They were one in their concern that the Lord's Supper be recovered as the chief service of the church's weekly worship. This constituted a radical demand. At the time of the Reformation very few Christians partook of communion more often than once a year. Many explanations for the decline and the eventual neglect of the practices of the early church may be made. However that may be, at the time of the Reformation the mass was celebrated daily but it had ceased to be a communal act in the sense in which the Roman Catholic Church seeks to encourage participation today. The mass was largely a thing to be observed and with the elevation of the Host the worshiper felt his "duty" had concluded. It was in order to restore a purified "mass" to the people that Luther and Calvin soon dealt with the question of worship. Luther, for instance, took the mass as it was then known and recast it in the German language, removing those elements which he thought were offensive to the new understanding of the Gospel through the Scriptures. It constituted a restoration of the Lord's Supper with communion by the people, together with preaching, as the chief act of worship.

Calvin desired to have the eucharist celebrated in each church every Sunday morning as the chief service. He was thwarted by the magistrates in Geneva who feared a return to Roman Catholic practices, as well as thwarted by the indolence of the people for whom this was a new venture involving the responsibility of preparing to receive communion weekly. Calvin was prevented from carrying out his liturgical reforms and accordingly made adjustments. He arranged to have the Lord's Supper celebrated in at least one church in Geneva each Sunday morning and, by this staggering of communion, to insure its observance each Sunday and its availability to the Christian community weekly. In addition, Calvin established a pattern of worship which had the structure of the eucharist, what is sometimes called a "dry communion." Although the "elements" of the communion were absent, the structure of worship pointed to a fulfilment in the breaking of bread and the sharing of the cup.

In the Anglican Reformation the eucharist was restored to centrality through the *Book of Common Prayer* in which the "Order of Holy Communion" was made the chief service. It should be noted that the order for holy communion was the only service in the Prayer Book which made specific provision for a sermon. Morning prayer and evening prayer were the "reformed" versions of the canonical offices. Scrutiny of their structure and historical inquiry reveal them to be daily services. They were never intended to constitute the weekly worship of a Christian congregation. Holy communion on Sunday was preceded often by morning prayer and the litany, but the Lord's Supper was basic to worship. In the absence of communicants, the service was truncated as with Calvin's suggestions, thereby becoming an ante-communion which still preserved the structure and focus of the eucharist.

The same concern for the centrality of the Lord's Supper can be found in the later manifestations of the continuing Reformation. Contrary to popular opinion, the English ancestors of the present-day Baptists and Congregationalists believed firmly in the importance of weekly observance of the Lord's Supper. By the time these movements arose, the habits of worship in the Church of England had lost the initial impetus and it was the Baptists and Congregationalists who represented a concern for frequent if not weekly celebration of the Lord's Supper.

Among the early Methodists the concern of John Wesley for frequent attendance at holy communion exerted influence. *The Eucharistic Hymns of John and Charles Wesley,* published recently, has made vivid Wesley's concern with the eucharist in terms which emphasize the corporate nature of the holy communion and the congregation's identification with its Lord who is both Priest and Victim. Apart from his seemingly "high church" attitude, in contrast to "high clerical" views, Wesley's preaching heightened interest in participation at the Lord's table to such an extent that parish priests in the Church of England were hard put. It has been suggested that the denial of communion to masses of people who responded to the evangelical and eucharistic preaching prompted the ordination of ministers who might preside at the table. It is intriguing to think that Methodism as a distinct denominational entity arose in some measure from the demand of Christian people to receive the communion denied them at the altars of local parish churches.

The illustration of the eucharistic concern in Protestantism can be extended to the United States. The Disciples of Christ is a group indigenous to America, although it is represented in Great Britain. Arising out of Thomas and Alexander Campbell's dismay that all Christians could not gather around the table of a common Lord, the movement displayed a concern for the eucharist and Christian unity. Although frustrated in part of its purpose, since the movement became a new denomination, its witness to the eucharist is manifested in each Disciples of Christ church where the Lord's Supper is celebrated every Sunday as an integral part of the congregation's worship.

This heritage has been lost in some instances and obscured or blunted in virtually every branch of the Reformation. Because of the infidelities of the children of the Reformation this heritage of a eucharist-centered worship has disappeared to such an extent that its recovery in our day is not recognized as such but as an unjustified intrusion upon Protestant principles. Renewed historical interest, however, is making Protestants aware of traditions and roots which can be the source of new life in worship.

Marvin P. Halverson

254　　*SINGULAR MEDICINE FOR ALL*
POOR SICK CREATURES

For albeit we feel in ourselves much frailty and wretchedness, as that we have not our faith perfect and constant as we ought, being many times ready to distrust God's goodness through our corrupt nature, and also that we are not so thoroughly given to serve God, neither have so fervent a zeal to set forth his glory as our duty requireth, feeling still such rebellion in ourselves, that we need daily to fight against the lusts of our flesh; yet, nevertheless, seeing that our Lord hath dealt thus mercifully with us, that he hath printed his Gospel in our hearts, so that we are preserved from falling into desperation and misbelief; and seeing also he hath indued us with a will and desire to renounce and withstand our own affections, with a longing for his righteousness and the keeping of his commandments, we may be now right well assured, that those defaults and manifold imperfections in us, shall be no hindrance at all against us, to cause him not [to] accept and impute as worthy to come to his spiritual table. For the end of our coming thither is not to make protestation that we are upright and just in our lives, but contrariwise. Let us consider, then, that this sacrament is a singular medicine for all poor sick creatures, a comfortable help to weak souls, and that our Lord requireth no other worthiness on our part, but that we unfeignedly acknowledge our naughtiness and imperfection.*

John Knox

255   SUPPORT FOR OUR SPIRITUAL LIFE

By commanding us to take, he signifies that he is ours; by commanding us to eat and drink, he signifies that he is become one substance with us. In saying that his body is given for us, and his blood shed for us, he shows that both are not so much his as ours, because he assumed and laid down both, not for his own advantage, but for our salvation. And it ought to be carefully observed that the principal and almost entire energy of the sacrament lies in these words, "which is given for you," "which is shed for you"—for otherwise it would avail us but little, that the body and blood of the Lord are distributed to us now, if they had not been once delivered for our redemption and salvation. Therefore they are represented to us by bread and wine, to teach us that they are not only ours, but are destined for the support of our spiritual life.

John Calvin

256   AN AGREEMENT OF MINDS

The Lord intended it to serve us as an exhortation, and no other could be better adapted to animate and influence us in the most powerful manner to purity and sanctity of life, as well as to charity, peace and concord. For there the Lord communicates his body to us in such a manner that he becomes completely one with us, and we become one with him. Now, as he has only one body, of which he makes us all partakers, it follows, of necessity, that, by such participation, we also are all made one body; and this union is represented by the bread which is exhibited in the sacrament. For as it is composed of many grains, mixed together in such a manner that one cannot be separated or distinguished from another—in the same manner we ought, likewise, to be connected and united together, by such an agreement of minds, as to admit of no dissension or division between us. . . . We have derived considerable benefit from the sacrament, if this thought be impressed and engraven upon our minds, that it is impossible for us to wound, despise, reject, injure, or in any way to offend one of our brethren, but we, at the same time, wound, despise, reject, injure, and offend Christ in him; that we have no discord with our brethren without being, at the same time, at variance with Christ; that we cannot love Christ without loving him in our brethren; that such care as we take of our own body, we ought to exercise the same care of our brethren, who are members of our body; that as no part of our body can be in any pain without every other part feeling correspondent sensations, so we ought not to suffer our brother to be afflicted with any calamity without our sympathizing in the same. Wherefore, it is not without reason that Augustine so frequently calls this sacrament "the bond of charity." For what more powerful stimulus could be employed to excite mutual charity among us, than when Christ, giving himself to us, not only invites us by his example mutually to devote ourselves to the promotion of one another's welfare, but also, by making himself common to all makes us all to be one with himself?

John Calvin

257 FELLOWSHIP WITH THE LIVING LORD

Central to Luther's conception of the Lord's Supper was the fellowship of Christians in and with the living Lord. This idea is prominent in the New Testament, particularly in the early chapters of the Book of the Acts, but it had been largely lost in the teaching of the medieval church. It fell to Luther to rediscover it, and in his early writings especially he gave it a conspicuous place. This rediscovery alone changed the whole aspect of worship. No longer could it remain merely a spectacle splendidly enacted as it were upon a stage; it must become a common action in which all shared. But if all were to share it, the worship must be intelligible, and to be wholly intelligible it must contain didactic elements. This end, Luther held, could be achieved only by retaining the celebration of the Lord's Supper as the central service of the church. . . . The result was that a weekly celebration of the Lord's Supper, with sermon and communion, became the early Lutheran tradition.

William D. Maxwell

258 THE EMPHASES OF ZWINGLI AND LUTHER

Zwingli, looking mainly at the medieval doctrine of the mass, taught: (1) The Lord's Supper is not a *repetition* of the sacrifice of Christ on the cross, but a *commemoration* of that sacrifice once offered up; and the elements are not a newly offered Christ, but the *signs* of the body and blood of the Christ who was once for all offered on Calvary. (2) That forgiveness for sin is not won by *partaking* in a newly offered Christ, but by *believing* in a Christ once offered up. (3) That the benefits of the work of Christ are always appropriated by faith, and that the atonement is so appropriated in the sacrament, whereby Christ becomes our food; but the food, being neither carnal nor corporeal, is not appropriated by the mouth, but by faith indwelling in the soul. Therefore, there is a real presence of Christ in the sacrament, but it is a spiritual presence, not a corporeal one. A real and living faith always involves the union of the believer with Christ, and therefore the real presence of Christ; and the presence of Christ, which is in every act of faith, is in the sacrament to the faithful partaker. (4) That while the Lord's Supper primarily refers to the sacrifice of Christ, and while the elements, bread and wine, are the symbols of the crucified body of Christ, the partaking of the elements is also a symbol and pledge of an ever-renewed living union with the risen Christ. (5) That as our Lord himself has specially warned his followers against thinking of feeding on him in any corporeal or carnal manner (John 6), the words of the institution cannot be taken in a strictly literal fashion, and the phrase, "This is my body," means, "This signifies my body." The fourth position had been rather implicitly held than explicitly stated.

Luther, looking mainly at the medieval doctrine of the eucharist, taught: (1) That the primary use of the sacrament was to bring believing communicants into direct touch with the living risen Christ. (2) That to this end there must be in the bread and wine the local presence of the glorified body of Christ, which he always conceived as "body extended in space"; the communicants, coming into touch with this body of Christ, have communion with him, such as his disciples had on earth and as his saints now have in heaven. (3) That this local presence of Christ does not presuppose any special priestly miracle, for, in virtue of its *ubiquity,* the glorified body of Christ is *everywhere* naturally, and therefore is in the bread and in the wine; this natural presence becomes a sacramental presence because of the promise of God attached to the reverent and believing partaking of the sacrament. (4) That communion with the living risen Christ implies the appropriation of the death of Christ, and of the atonement won by his death; but this last thought of Luther's, which is Zwingli's first thought, lies implicitly in his teaching without being dwelt upon.

Thomas M. Lindsay

S. THE GENIUS OF DA VINCI

259 *RECAPTURING THE TRUE SIGNIFICANCE*

In Milan, Italy, Leonardo da Vinci's masterpiece "The Last Supper" is painted on the north wall of the little refectory of a convent. There it has stood for four hundred and fifty years, facing the wind and dampness, with its survival threatened by the indiscriminate ravages of war.

The years have had their effect. Dampness has blistered the wall; the blisters have been flattened and replaced with plaster and paint by well-meaning but less expert hands. The original colors have been overlaid with imitation.

In recent years a new shellac was injected into the rotting wall which dried up the mold that had accumulated on the painting. Then someone proposed that the layers of colors—at least five—be chipped away and Leonardo's original work be rediscovered. Over a three-year period the restorer worked with a surgeon's scalpel, completing the project in 1954. Art critics exclaimed in amazement at what they saw. Da Vinci's great mastery and authentic recapture of the gospel spirit was at last really apparent, after centuries of misrepresentation. Said one: "I felt that I had touched bottom. The figures emerged as from a mist, large and imposing. Space was full of their presence."

The sacrament that grew out of the Last Supper has in many respects suffered the same fate as da Vinci's painting. It has been overlaid with restrictions and interpretations that have been the clumsy effort of men to preserve its meaning; they have done what the five layers of color have done to "The Last Supper"—obscured its real significance. We need the scalpel that will help us recapture the true significance of the communion.

George Laird Hunt

260 *CENTRAL BEAUTY*

A friend who had come to see da Vinci's great picture, "The Last Supper," remarked first of all the brilliancy of the silver cup. Da Vinci took his brush and painted the cup out. He would have nothing in his picture which drew attention away from its central Figure. . . . The original sketch of the face of Jesus made for "The Last Supper" still exists. In that study, da Vinci has embodied in undying beauty the sad, tender grace which he read in the countenance of Jesus.

Richard Roberts

261   THE MASTER'S FACE

When Leonardo da Vinci was painting for the *Cenacolo,* the great canvas of "The Last Supper," he labored for eighteen years on the head of Christ. The first cartoon he made was from the model of an artisan's son, a brown-faced, ruddy child of earth, humanity raised and enhanced until the boy of the street was like and unlike the common run of men. This face was the face of Christ, the Son of Man. He would make a powerful appeal on the great canvas, a fellow sufferer, a fellow aspirant, a fellow man, defeated and yet victorious in the strife.

But Leonardo was not satisfied and he drew another face, austere, detached, touched with the feeling of our infirmities, yet immensely removed. This was the face of Christ, the Son of God. This face would appeal to reflective or philosophical minds, those who needed reason and logic to undergird the leap of faith. But Leonardo was never satisfied, and the face was never finally painted. Both cartoons were Christ, both would lead men unto God, but Jesus could not be altogether known nor fully grasped, and Leonardo knew it to be better so.

George Stewart

262   INNER ALTAR OF THE HEART

[Da Vinci's] last three years were spent in France in the service of the King of France. Having become old, he lay sick for many months, and, finding himself near death, he wrought diligently to make himself acquainted with the Catholic ritual and with the path of religion, so records Giorgio Vassari. He then confessed with great penitence and many tears, and, although he could not support himself on his feet, yet, being sustained in the arms of his servants and friends, he devoutly received the holy communion while out of bed. Thus did he who had presented a masterpiece in art on the sacrament to a Christ-seeking world wait till he was near death's door to partake of its spirit. He had barred himself from this sacrament. Barred by his own hands! He had exposed himself to its *exterior* form rather than to its *interior* force. Pity the modern

Christian who only partakes of the exterior of communion without its soulful interior grace and influence. The real artistry of the sacrament cannot be painted with brush and oils. One must go deeper than that; yea, to the inner altars of the mystic heart of man.

Edward Jeffries Rees

T. THE HEART'S PREPARATION

263   SELF-EXAMINATION: AN EXERCISE
BEFORE COMMUNION

But let a man examine himself, and so let him eat of that bread, and drink of that cup. I CORINTHIANS 11:28

The chief thing is that we should examine ourselves, should be prepared to receive the blessing of communion. There is no emphasis laid on any particular method of examination. You will notice that St. Paul does not give any particular directions, does not draw up a practical scheme of preparation at all. Any such rules would become formal, and might be a burden to the over-sensitive, scrupulous soul, and would only soothe the soul of the mere formalist into duller and smugger self-satisfaction. The truth is that there are no formal rules which are of universal applicability. The things which are demanded are sincerity and seriousness.

Hugh Black

264   EXAMINATION OF MOTIVES

A man, before he . . . begins to examine himself, would do well *to examine himself as to why he is going to examine himself,* and to ask, Why am I going to do this? Because it is my interest? Because I think I shall gain more safety for my soul? Because I hope it will give me more chance of pleasure and glory in the next world? But, if so, have I the mind of Christ? For he did *not* think of his own interest, his own gain, his own pleasure, his own glory. How is this, then? I confess that the root of all my faults is selfishness. Shall I examine into my own selfishness for a selfish end—to get safety and pleasure by it hereafter? I confess that the very glory of Christ is that there is no selfishness in him. Shall I think over the sufferings of the unselfish Christ for a selfish end—to get something by it after I die? I am too apt already to make myself the center, round which all the world must turn: to care for everything only as far as it does *me* good or harm. Shall I make myself the center round which heaven is to turn? Shall I think of God and of Christ only as far as it will profit *me?*

Charles Kingsley

265   *SOLEMN SELF-EXAMINATION*

Let a man prove himself, and so let him eat of the bread, and drink of the cup.   I CORINTHIANS 11:28

These words are blazoned over the portal of every place where the members of the Christian fellowship gather together to observe the holy ordinance of the communion. The places vary as to situation and as to structure, from the stately cathedral to the lowliest cottage. The methods may be as far apart as that of a solemn ritual and that of a simple rite. These, after all, are the incidental, indeed, the accidental, things. In themselves they do not matter. They are neither essentially right or wrong. Finally, the differences matter nothing. Let every man be fully persuaded in his own mind, and let him be true to that persuasion, while he respects the persuasions of others which he does not share.

The supreme thing, the essential thing, is the sacred act of communion, the practice of a communion which is constant. It is the act in which the soul is called upon to exercise the highest function of its ransomed nature, that of worship in its purity, and in which it is strengthened for the exercise by the fullest realization of fellowship with the Risen Lord. All that reveals the supreme importance of this injunction. Before the hour of fellowship and of worship, there should be solemn self-examination. It should not take place in the service, but before it. The Table of the Lord is not the place for the confession of sin; that must precede it. The absolution of our High Priest is to be sought and found before we enter into the holy of holies to offer to him the sacrifices of our adoration. So we are to eat the bread and drink the cup as cleansed worshippers, having no more consciousness of sins. It is at our peril that we neglect such preparation.

G. Campbell Morgan

266   *RETURN TO CHRIST*

If you have wandered from the Christ within the soul, this is our time —this is our place—of return. Again and again, after every failure, we must come back with contrition but without despair. Here is the rendez-vous of our fidelity; here our communion once more; here the divine guide with whose will we are henceforth to harmonize our own. This hour is to be hospitable to the holiest messenger of God; to make ready the guest chamber in the upper dwelling of our hearts and to shut out, amid the converse of blessed thoughts, the voices of men and the threatenings of sorrow. Let pure and perfect trust fill all the room; let the Judas-element in our soul rise and quickly pass into the night and the love that remains rest there with freer surrender upon the form of heavenly sanctity.

James Martineau

267   *TO GET RID OF OURSELVES*

That examination of ourselves which the church, following St. Paul, enjoins upon those who would eat of that bread and drink of that cup, is not, I apprehend, an examination into our own state of mind, to see whether we have internal qualifications for coming to the feast, but an examination whether we want to get rid of ourselves, whether we would really have a Deliverer, if we could find him, from all that degrades us, a Friend in whom we could inherit that righteousness and truth which we have not, and are never meant to have till we forget ourselves and seek them in him. It is certainly a profane thing to come to a sacrament which tells us of fellowship with a righteous Being, if we would rather be without such fellowship; which tells us of a new and noble nature, if we prefer our old and base nature. And therefore to examine ourselves whether we be in the faith—that is to say, whether we count Christ to be the Deliverer and the Giver of a new life to mankind, which the Bible says he is—must certainly be a most desirable preparation for the marriage supper.

Frederick Denison Maurice

268   *BEFORE THE FEAST*

It is not the preparation of two or three days that can render a person capable of this banquet: for in this feast all Christ, and Christ's passion, and all his graces, the blessings and effects of his sufferings, are conveyed. Nothing can fit us for this but what can unite us to Christ, and obtain of him to present our needs to his heavenly Father: this sacrament can not otherwise be celebrated but upon the same terms on which we may hope for pardon and heaven itself. . . .

When the day of the feast is come, lay aside all cares and impertinences of the world, and remember that this is thy soul's day, a day of traffic and intercourse with heaven. Arise early in the morning.

1. Give God thanks for the approach of so great a blessing.
2. Confess thine own unworthiness to admit so divine a guest.

3. Then remember and deplore thy sins, which have made thee so unworthy.

4. Then confess God's goodness, and take sanctuary there, and upon him place thy hopes.

5. And invite him to thee with renewed acts of love, of holy desire, of hatred of his enemy, sin.

6. Make oblation to thyself wholly to be disposed by him, to the obedience of him, to his providence and possession, and pray him to enter and dwell there forever.

And after this, with joy and holy fear, and the forwardness of love, address thyself to the receiving of him, to whom, and by whom, and for whom all faith, and all hope, and all love in the whole catholic church, both in heaven and earth, is designed.

Jeremy Taylor

269 *IN WANT OF DISCERNMENT*

He that eateth and drinketh, eateth and drinketh judgment unto himself if he discern not the body. . . . But if we discerned ourselves we should not be judged. I CORINTHIANS 11:29, 31

It is because of [the] limitation of our minds that certain times have been set apart in which we deliberately break through the familiar outer aspect of things; times when we cease to be concerned with the work and the food and the beauty of the earth in and for themselves, but look through them to what lies beyond; and, to guide our aspirations at these times, certain ordinances have been established, one pre-eminently in which the familiar truth that man lives by bread becomes a symbol of the greater truth that he lives by the Word of God. It was precisely the failure to make the right use of this means of grace to which St. Paul attributes the spiritual sloth of the Corinthians. He charges them with want of discernment in the act of holy communion. This sacrament was, as it were, a window made for them from earth into heaven, and they closed and darkened it from within. They made its sacredness common, treating it as an ordinary meal, instead of receiving it as the touchstone by which all familiar things were to be seen in their true meaning, the key to the interpretation of human life. Instead of trying to carry the truth learned at the eucharist into everyday life, they brought the half-truths of every day into their eucharist. Instead of interpreting the world by that, they interpreted that by their common experience of the world.

H. C. Beeching

270   *CHRIST-IN-MAN*

As John the Baptist was the original messenger dedicated to preparing the way for the Christ's earthly coming, so are you and I created as messengers dedicated to preparing the way for his coming into our hearts, as well as into the hearts of the brethren around us, near and far. Which fact reminds one of that heroic statue of Christ in the yard of Trinity Church, Boston. The wonder of that statue lies not only in the glory of the Lord there represented, but also in the presence of Phillips Brooks, who is depicted as standing out in front of our Lord, preparing his way. Compared with the figure of the Christ, Phillips Brooks is small and ineffectual-looking. Taken alone, no one knew better than Brooks that he counted for little in the scheme of things. But one of the significant points about this dual statue is that the Christ has placed his out-stretched hand on Phillips Brooks' shoulder. In short, the great things that Christ was effecting, Brooks was preparing the way for! He was in front of his Lord, plowing the soil as it were, so that his Lord might plant the divine seed.

Even that perpetual miracle, the holy communion, began as a Christ-plus-man action. It still continues as a Christ-with-man miracle, and will go on as such until the end of time. On the very night of the institution of the Last Supper itself, the Lord did not come into those blessed elements of bread and of wine until his disciples had made an oblation, so that he could pour himself into it. It is always required of a Christian steward that he offer back to Christ something of the gift originally vouchsafed him by his Lord, but only after the steward has injected something of his own labor and love into it. Then it is that the Lord of life infuses those given elements and returns them to the stewards in the form of the divine nourishment of his body and blood. That is implicitly why the disciples were given the prior tasks of securing and preparing the upper room.

John E. Large

IV. A Treasury of Communion Poetry

Amidst us our Belovèd stands,
  And bids us view his piercèd hands;
Points to the wounded feet and side,
  Blest emblems of the crucified.

What food luxurious loads the board
  When, at his table, sits the Lord!
The wine how rich, the bread how sweet
  When Jesus deigns the guests to meet!

If now, with eyes defiled and dim,
  We see the signs, but see not him;
O, may his love the scales displace,
  And bid us see him face to face!

Thou glorious Bridegroom of our hearts,
  Thy present smile a heaven imparts!
O, lift the veil, if veil there be,
  Let every saint thy glory see!

Charles H. Spurgeon

272   *DIM TRACTS OF TIME DIVIDE*

Dim tracts of time divide
  Those golden days from me;
Thy voice comes strange o'er years of change;
  How can I follow thee?

Comes faint and far thy voice
  From vales of Galilee;
Thy vision fades in ancient shades;
  How should we follow thee?

Francis Turner Palgrave

273   *ALL PRAISE TO HIM OF NAZARETH*

All praise to him of Nazareth,
  The Holy One who came,
For love of man, to die a death
  Of agony and shame.

Dark was the grave; but since he lay
  Within its dreary cell,
The beams of heaven's eternal day
  Upon its threshold dwell.

He grasped the iron veil, he drew
  Its gloomy folds aside,
And opened, to his followers' view,
  The glorious world they hide.

In tender memory of his grave
  The mystic bread we take,
And muse upon the life he gave
  So freely for our sake.

A boundless love he bore mankind;
  Oh, may at least a part
Of that strong love descend and find
  A place in every heart.

                                        William Cullen Bryant

274   *THE SACRAMENT*

"This is my body, which is given for you;
  Do this," he said, "and break, rememb'ring me."
O Lamb of God, our Paschal off'ring true,
  To us the Bread of Life each moment be.

"This is my blood, for sins' remission shed";
  He spake, and passed the cup of blessing round;
So let us drink, and, on life's fullness fed,
  With heavenly joy each quickening pulse shall bound.

Some will betray thee—"Master, is it I?"
  Leaning upon thy love, we ask in fear—
Ourselves mistrusting, earnestly we cry
  To thee, the Strong, for strength, when sin is near.

But round us fall the evening shadows dim;
  A saddened awe pervades our darkening sense;
In solemn choir we sing the parting hymn,
  And hear thy voice, "Arise, let us go hence."

Charles L. Ford

275   *REMEMBER ME*

"Remember me," the Savior said
  On that forsaken night,
When from his side the nearest fled,
  And death was close in sight.

Through all the following ages' track,
  The world remembers yet;
And love and worship gazes back,
  And never can forget.

We see his word along our way;
  And see his light above;
Remember when we strive and pray,
  Remember when we love.

Nathaniel Langdon Frothingham

276   *REMEMBRANCE*

The sun lay warm on tawny fields
  Of wheat in Galilee,
Where lilies swayed and winds were soft
  Beside a summer sea.

There purple vineyards climbed the slopes
  And fragrance filled the air,
While flocks of doves on silver wings
  Ascended like a prayer.

Was he, perhaps, remembering
    The peace of wheat and vine
That night he made a sacrament
    Of bread and wine?

Leslie Savage Clark

277   *ACCORDING TO THY GRACIOUS WORD*

According to thy gracious Word,
    In meek humility,
This will I do, my dying Lord,
    I will remember thee.

Thy body, broken for my sake,
    My bread from heaven shall be;
Thy testamental cup I take
    And thus remember thee.

*

Remember thee and all thy pains,
    And all thy love to me!
Yea, while a breath, a pulse remains,
    Will I remember thee.

And, when these failing lips grow dumb,
    And mind and memory flee,
When thou shalt in thy kingdom come,
    Jesus, remember me.

James Montgomery

278   *AND COULD'ST THOU, LORD*

And could'st thou, Lord, thy thanks express
In prospect of thy deep distress?
And at the table, spread to show
Thy symbols of thy coming woe.

And could'st thou bless thy God on high,
That he had sent thee thus to die,
And for our sins to give thee up,
To drink wrath's overwhelming cup?

O! what a love must thine have been!
To *praise* in view of such a scene!
When broken bread, and poured out wine,
Portrayed those bitter woes of thine.

William Grant

279 *From* WHEN JESUS WASHED THE FEET OF JUDAS

What were his thoughts,
What grieving tore his heart,
What pity drove him to the bitter part,
When he, the Lord, fell on his knees
To wash the feet of Judas?

None saw a frown,
Nay, did not he, the traitor, feel
A tender pressure on his sordid heel,
When he, the Lord, fell on his knees
To wash the feet of Judas?

Straight from his heart
What passion burst and pled
To call a blinded comrade from the dead,
When he, the Lord, fell on his knees
To wash the feet of Judas?

Ralph Spaulding Cushman

280

THE SOP

It was no enemy which did this wrong,
    But one who held with him communion sweet;
Chosen and trusted, taught and cherished long—
    Had he not humbly stooped to wash his feet?
This was the man! and now the hour was nigh;
And Judas, who betrayed, said, "Master, is it I?"

But when from out the dish the sop he drew
    Which to the traitor his dark soul betrayed;
All bitterness from all the herbs that grew
    Since man lost paradise, that sop conveyed.

The bruised palms of more than mortal death
Combine to furnish forth the Savior's haroseth!

Author Unknown (1856)

281   *MY BROKEN BODY*

My broken body thus I give
For you, for all; take, eat, and live;
And oft the sacred rite renew
That brings my wondrous love to view.

*

My blood I thus pour forth, he cries,
To cleanse the soul in sin that lies;
In this the covenant is sealed,
And heaven's eternal grace revealed.

With love to man this cup is fraught;
Let all partake the sacred draught;
Through latest ages let it pour,
In memory of my dying hour.

John Morrison

282   *DO THIS*

I give my body for your sake;
  If needs must be,
Your bodies also you must break
  In memory of me.

I give my blood, in pain and bitter loss;
  You, too, must spill
Your life-blood, if I call you from the cross
  To do my Father's will.

Godfrey Fox Bradby

283   *THE LAST SUPPER*

What song sang the twelve with the Savior
  When finish'd the sacrament wine?
Were they bow'd and subdued in behavior,
  Or bold as made bold with a sign?

Were the hairy breasts strong and defiant?
  Were the naked arms brawny and strong?
Were the bearded lips lifted reliant,
  Thrust forth and full sturdy with song!

What sang they? What sweet song of Zion
  With Christ in their midst like a crown?
While here sat Saint Peter, the lion;
  And there like a lamb, with head down,

Sat Saint John, with his silken and raven
  Rich hair on his shoulders, and eyes
Lifting up to the faces unshaven
  Like a sensitive child's in surprise.

Was the song as strong fishermen swinging
  Their nets full of hope to the sea?
Or low, like the ripple-wave, singing
  Sea-songs on their loved Galilee?

Were they sad with foreshadow of sorrows,
  Like the birds that sing low when the breeze
Is tip-toe with a tale of to-morrows,—
  Of earthquakes and sinking of seas?

Ah! soft was their song as the waves are
  That fall in low musical moans;
And sad I should say as the winds are
  That blow by the white gravestones.

Joaquin Miller

284   *TWO CHALICES*

There was a chalice in the ancient East
Unhallowed by the Master of the Feast;
It did not catch the sacramental tide
That welled from Jesus' lacerated side,
Nor lure Sir Galahad to seek the shrine
Whence glowed its radiance and flowed its wine.
It was abandoned at a village well
When once a passing stranger stopped to tell

Of founts of living water that may spring
Within the soul, and make the spirit sing.

Two sacred chalices I shall acclaim:
One from an upper room; of lesser fame
One from a well, illumined by his name.

Edwin McNeill Poteat

285   *THE ROAD TO EMMAUS*

Twilight. And on a dusty ribboned way,
Out from Jerusalem, two travelers walked.
Gray shadows touched their feet, but deeper lay
The shadows in their hearts. They softly talked
Of days just passed, of hopeless days in view,
Of boats, of nets, the while their eyes were dim,
Of Galilee, the work they used to do;
Their voices often stilled, remembering Him.

A stranger also walked that way, and when
They sensed his nearness, some new sympathy
Assuaged their grief. Old hopes came warm again
As, in the dusk, he kept them company . . .
Thus, through the troubled twilight of today
Emmaus road has stretched its shining thread,
And still Christ walks beside men on the way,
To hold the light of hope, to break the bread.

Ida Norton Munson

286   *EMMAUS*

They, with a stranger, broke the bread:
    "Do this; remember me!"
And all at once they saw—not dead—
    His true reality:
The outstretched hands, the love shed wide
Of him that had, yet had not died—
    And all the Life that was to be.

Laurence Housman

287   *O THOU WHO THIS MYSTERIOUS BREAD*

O thou who this mysterious bread
    Didst in Emmaus break,
Return, herewith our souls to feed,
    And to thy followers speak.

Unseal the volume of thy grace,
    Apply the gospel word,
Open our eyes to see thy face,
    Our hearts to know the Lord.

Of thee we commune still, and mourn
    Till thou the veil remove;
Talk with us, and our hearts shall burn
    With flames of fervent love.

Enkindle now the heavenly zeal,
    And make thy mercy known,
And give our pardon'd souls to feel
    That God and love are one.

                            Charles Wesley

288   *VIA LUCIS*

And have the bright immensities
    Received our risen Lord
Where light-years frame the Pleiades
    And point Orion's sword?

Do flaming suns his footsteps trace
    Through corridors sublime,
The Lord of interstellar space
    And Conqueror of time?

The heaven that hides him from our sight
    Knows neither near nor far:
An altar candle sheds its light
    As surely as a star;

And where his loving people meet
  To share the gift divine,
There stands he with unhurrying feet;
  There heavenly splendors shine.

Howard Chandler Robbins

289   *From THE MAN OF NAZARETH*

O Friend and Brother, draw more near
  The while thy festival we keep;
Diviner shall our lives appear
  Held fast in thy high fellowship.

Frederick L. Hosmer

290   *From THE INVITATION*

Come ye yourselves apart and rest awhile,
  Weary, I know it, of the press and throng,
Wipe from your brow the sweat and dust of toil,
  And in my quiet strength again be strong.

*

Come ye and rest; the journey is too great,
  And ye will faint beside the way and sink;
The Bread of Life is here for you to eat
  And here for you the Wine of Love to drink.

Edward Henry Bickersteth

291   *THE QUEST*

If in the press of every day
The holy chalice slips away;
If in the treadmill of my toil
My lamps are dry of festal oil;
If in the desert waste of things
I find no wells, no limpid springs:
  Lord, touch with dew my parching heart,
  Anoint it ere it crack apart.
If in my own felicity
I walk as one who does not see;
If in a tangled underbrush
I move, and know not what I crush;

If in an avalanche of care
I use not mountain-moving prayer:
    Grant me no highway to the Grail—
    But light me, Lord, to find a trail.

Georgia Harkness

292   *ALAS, MY GOD*

Alas, my God, that we should be
    Such strangers to each other!
O that as friends we might agree,
    And walk and talk together!

May I taste that communion, Lord,
    Thy people have with thee?
Thy Spirit daily talks with them,
    O let it talk with me!

Thomas Shepherd

293   *LOVE*

Love bade me welcome: yet my soul drew back,
    Guiltie of dust and sinne.
But quick-ey'd Love, observing me grow slack
    From my first entrance in,
Drew nearer to me, sweetly questioning,
    If I lack'd any thing.

A guest, I answer'd, worthy to be here:
    Love said, you shall be he.
I the unkinde, ungratefull? Ah my deare,
    I cannot look on thee.
Love took my hand, and smiling did reply,
    Who made the eyes but I?

Truth Lord, but I have marr'd them: let my shame
    Go where it doth deserve.
And know you not, sayes Love, who bore the blame?
    My deare, then I will serve.
You must sit down, sayes Love, and taste my meat:
    So I did sit and eat.

George Herbert

294   *SACRAMENT*

At many an altar I have knelt
And tasted bread and drank of wine:
The broken body and the blood
Of One who gave his life for mine.

But there is other wine to drink,
And there is other bread to break:
The bread of labor, and the sweet
Bright wine of rest I nightly take.

The wine of Love is poured for me,
And daily Love and I break bread.
Not only on the Sabbath day
Are sacramental tables spread.

But every day within my heart,
White damask gleams, and wine cups shine;
I pass the bread of charity,
Through sympathy I share my wine.

                                    Grace Noll Crowell

295   *THE DESPONDING SOUL'S WISH*

My spirit longeth for thee,
    Within my troubled breast;
Altho' I be unworthy
    Of so divine a Guest.

Of so divine a Guest,
    Unworthy tho' I be;
Yet has my heart no rest,
    Unless it come from thee.

Unless it come from thee,
    In vain I look around;
In all that I can see,
    No rest is to be found.

No rest is to be found,
    But in thy blessed love;

O! let my wish be crown'd,
And send it from above!

John Byrom

296   *From WELCOME TO THE TABLE*

This is the feast of heavenly wine,
    And God invites to sup;
The juices of the living Vine
    Were press'd to fill the cup.

Oh! bless the Savior, ye that eat,
    With royal dainties fed;
Not heaven affords a costlier treat,
    For Jesus is the bread.

William Cowper

297   *THE SPREAD TABLE*

Where'er I be, Lord, spread for me
Thy table with its holy fare,
Then, though my lot be slenderness,
And my tent but the wilderness,
Full amply plenished I shall be,
    Since thou art there.

And wilt thou break the bread for me?
For me pour out the sacred wine?
And as we eat and drink wilt thou
Renew in me the holy vow,
And fill me with new love for thee,
    Since I am thine?

Not the spread table, nor the wine,
Nor the sweet breaking of the bread,
That makes the feast,—but that we meet
Together here in commune sweet
With thee, and by thy Grace Divine,
    We all are fed.

And when we leave thy table, Lord,
And go into the world again,
Help us to carry with us there
The savour of that holy fare,
And prove the virtue of thy Word
    To other men.

John Oxenham

298   *From THE KING OF LOVE*

Thou spread'st a table in my sight;
    Thy unction grace bestoweth;
And O, what transport and delight
    From thy pure chalice floweth!

Henry W. Baker

299   *DO THIS IN REMEMBRANCE OF ME*

Here, O my Lord, I see thee face to face;
    Here would I touch and handle things unseen;
Here grasp with firmer hand the eternal grace,
    And all my weariness upon thee lean.

Here would I feed upon the Bread of God;
    Here drink with thee the Royal Wine of Heaven;
Here would I lay aside each earthly load;
    Here taste afresh the calm of sin forgiven.

This is the hour of banquet and of song,
    This is the heavenly table spread for me;
Here let me feast, and feasting, still prolong
    The brief bright hour of fellowship with thee.

Too soon we rise; the symbols disappear;
    The feast, though not the love, is past and gone;
The bread and wine remove; but thou art here,
    Nearer than ever; still my Shield and Sun.

I have no help but thine; nor do I need
    Another arm but thine to lean upon;

It is enough, my Lord; enough, indeed,
  My strength is in thy might, thy might alone.

         *

Mine is the sin, but thine the righteousness;
  Mine is the guilt, but thine the cleansing blood;
Here is my robe, my refuge, and my peace,
  Thy blood, thy righteousness, O Lord my God.

         *

Feast after feast thus comes, and passes by;
  Yet, passing, points to the glad feast above,
Giving sweet foretaste of the festal joy,
  The Lamb's great bridal feast of bliss and love.

Horatius Bonar

300   *THEE WE ADORE*

    Thee we adore, O hidden Savior, thee,
    Who in thy supper with us deign'st to be;
    Both flesh and spirit in thy presence fail,
    Yet here thy presence we devoutly hail.

         *

    O Christ, whom now beneath a veil we see,
    May what we thirst for soon our portion be,
    To gaze on thee unveiled, and see thy face,
    The vision of thy glory and thy grace.

Thomas Aquinas; tr. J. R. Woodford

301   *HOW HAPPY ARE THY SERVANTS, LORD*

    How happy are thy servants, Lord,
      Who thus remember thee!
    What tongue can tell our sweet accord,
      Our perfect harmony?

    Who thy mysterious supper share,
      Here at thy table fed,
    Many, and yet but one are we,
      One undivided bread.

One with the living Bread divine
   Which now by faith we eat,
Our hearts, and minds, and spirits join,
   And all in Jesus meet.

So dear the tie where souls agree
   In Jesu's dying love;
Then only can it closer be,
   When all are join'd above.

Charles Wesley

302   *UPPER ROOM COMMUNION HYMN*

To thee I come, thou gracious Christ
   In deep humility.
As in the hallowed Upper Room
   I would remember thee.

I know I am unworthy, Lord,
   Of all thy love so free,
And I pray that thou wilt forgive
   As I remember thee.

The broken bread, thy body torn,
   Bread of life is to me,
For thou dost feed my famished soul
   As I remember thee.

Thy shed blood as the wine outpoured
   I believe was for me.
Lord, may thy spirit fill my soul
   As I remember thee.

Frederick B. Morley

303   *AND SO WE COME*

And so we come; O draw us to thy feet,
   Most patient Savior, who canst love us still;
And by this food, so awful and so sweet,
   Deliver us from every touch of ill:

In thine own service make us glad and free,
And grant us never more to part with thee.

William Bright

304   *DECK THYSELF, MY SOUL*

Deck thyself, my soul, with gladness,
Leave thy gloomy haunts of sadness;
Come into the daylight's splendor,
There with joy thy praises render
Unto him whose grace unbounded
Hath this wondrous banquet founded:
High o'er all the heavens he reigneth
Yet to dwell with thee he deigneth.

Traditional hymn

305   *WHAT HE DID AT SUPPER SEATED*

What he did at supper seated,
Christ ordained to be repeated,
  His memorial ne'er to cease:
And, his word for guidance taking,
Bread and wine we hallow, making
  Thus his sacrifice of peace.

Author Unknown

306   *NOT WORTHY, LORD*

Not worthy, Lord, to gather up the crumbs
With trembling hand, that from thy table fall,
A weary, heavy-laden sinner comes
To plead thy promise and obey thy call.

*

I hear thy voice: thou bid'st me come and rest;
I come, I kneel, I clasp thy piercèd feet;
Thou bid'st me take my place, a welcome guest,
Among thy saints, and of thy banquet eat.

My praise can only breathe itself in prayer,
My prayer can only lose itself in thee;
Dwell thou forever in my heart, and there,
Lord, let me sup with thee; sup thou with me.

Edward Henry Bickersteth

307 *COMMUNION*

Oh heart, be humble and adore,
And feast on hunger, lacking more.
For in desire you shall discover
How Love comes searching for its lover.

Eleanor Slater

308 *THE SACRAMENT*

The symbols of thy sacrament
 I fain would make them mine;
Thy body is the broken bread,
 Thy blood the poured out wine;
What blessed significance they hold,
 What graciousness divine.

The sorrow of thy sacrament,
 That also should be mine:
The washing of the dusty feet
 In sad humility,
The traitor scowl, the bloody sweat
 Of lone Gethsemane.

The blessings of thy sacrament
 Are with thy servant still:
Acceptance of the solemn cup,
 The doing of God's will,
The finishing of sacrifice
 Upon the holy hill.

The glories of thy sacrament
 Through all the nations run:

The Father's loving majesty,
   The kingdom of the Son,
The radiance of the Holy Ghost—
   Supernal Three in One.

The presence of thy sacrament
   Is with me all the days:
The strengthening bread, the solemn cup,
   The hymn of lofty praise,
The high communion that exalts
   My lowly trodden ways.

The promise of thy sacrament
   Glows ever through the night,
The hope of heaven shining clear
   Upon the yearning sight,
The day-star rising in the East
   With sure and surer light.

O Savior of the sacrament,
   Redeemer ever blest,
My risen Lord, my throned King,
   My sacrifice confessed,
In thee I live, in thee I trust,
   And oh! in thee I rest.

Amos R. Wells

309   *O BREAD TO PILGRIMS GIVEN*

O bread to pilgrims given,
   Richer than angels eat,
O manna sent from heaven,
   For heaven-born natures meet!
Give us, for thee long pining,
   To eat till richly filled;
Till, earth's delights resigning,
   Our ev'ry wish is stilled!

*

Jesus, this feast receiving,
  We thee unseen adore;
Thy faithful Word believing,
  We take, and doubt no more.

Author Unknown; tr. Ray Palmer

310   *A PRAYER FOR THE PRESENCE OF CHRIST*

Reveal thy presence now, O Lord,
  As in the upper room of old;
Break thou our bread, grace thou our board,
  And keep our hearts from growing cold.

Thomas Tiplady

311   *LORD JESUS CHRIST, WE HUMBLY PRAY*

Lord Jesus Christ, we humbly pray
That we may feed on thee today;
Beneath these forms of bread and wine,
Enrich us with thy grace divine.

*

One bread, one cup, one body, we
United by our life in thee,
Thy love proclaim till thou shalt come,
To bring thy scattered loved ones home.

Henry E. Jacobs

312   *From JESUS, THOU JOY OF LOVING HEARTS*

We taste theee, O thou living Bread,
  And long to feast upon thee still;
We drink of thee, the Fountain-head,
  And thirst our souls from thee to fill.

Our restless spirits yearn for thee,
  Where'er our changeful lot is cast;
Glad, when thy gracious smile we see,
  Blest, when our faith can hold thee fast.

Bernard of Clairvaux; tr. Ray Palmer

313   *BREAK THOU THE BREAD OF LIFE*

> Break thou the bread of life,
>   Dear Lord, to me,
> As thou didst break the loaves
>   Beside the sea;
> Beyond the sacred page
>   I seek thee, Lord,
> My spirit pants for thee,
>   O living Word.
>
> Bless thou the bread of life,
>   To me, to me,
> As thou didst bless the bread
>   By Galilee;
> Then shall all bondage cease,
>   All fetters fall;
> And I shall find my peace,
>   My all in all.

Mary A. Lathbury

314   *BREAD OF THE WORLD*

> Bread of the world in mercy broken,
> Wine of the soul in mercy shed,
> By whom the words of life were spoken,
> And in whose death our sins are dead;
>
> Look on the heart by sorrow broken,
> Look on the tears by sinners shed;
> And be thy feast to us the token
> That by thy grace our souls are fed.

Reginald Heber

315   *BREAD*

> He knew what hunger a man can feel,
>   So he broke the fishes and bread
> That the weary thousands who followed him
>   Might be strengthened and fed.

He knew what hunger a soul can feel,
  Sharing the husks with swine,
So he gave his broken body and blood
  For bread and wine.

Leslie Savage Clark

316 *LET THY BLOOD*

Let thy blood in mercy poured,
  Let thy gracious body broken,
Be to me, O gracious Lord,
  Of thy boundless love the token:
Thou didst give thyself for me;
Now I give myself to thee.

John Brownlie

317 *From MY BELOVED IS MINE*

He is my Altar; I, his holy Place;
  I am his guest; and he, my living food;
I'm his by penitence; he mine by grace;
  I'm his by purchase; he is mine, by blood;
  He's my supporting elm; and I his vine;
Thus I my best-beloved's am; thus he is mine.

Francis Quarles

318 *TABLE TRIPLETS*

Year by year, the Man Divine,
Where the southern sunlights shine,
Turns the water into wine.

Year by year, he makes the corn,
Under ground in burial borne
Rise with him on Easter morn.

Whence, ere one year's store is spent
Bread and wine afresh are sent
For the next year's sacrament.

W. B. Robertson

319   *THE SACRAMENT OF FOOD*

Each meal should be a sacramental feast,—
A eucharist each breaking of the bread,
Wherein we meet again our Great High Priest,
And pledge new troth to our exalted Head.

For all we eat doth come of sacrifice,—
Life out of death,—since all we eat must yield
Life for our living,—and yet, nothing dies,
But in the giving finds its life fulfilled.

The wheat, the plant, the beast, and man, all give,
Each of their best, God's purpose to maintain,
And all subserve the end for which all live,
And pass,—to live more worthily again.

John Oxenham

320   *From COMMUNION*

One Christ we feed upon, one living Christ,
    Who once was dead, but lives forever now;
One is the cup of blessing which we bless,
    True symbol of the blood which from the cross did flow.

*

My life, my everlasting life art thou,
    My health, my joy, my strength I owe to thee;
Because thou livest, I shall also live,
    And where thou art in glory, there I too shall be.

Horatius Bonar

321   *THAT THEY ALL MAY BE ONE*

Thou who, at thy first eucharist, didst pray
    That all thy church might be forever one,
Grant us at every eucharist to say
    With longing heart and soul, "Thy will be done."
Oh may we all one bread, one body be,
Through this blest sacrament of unity.

For all thy church, O Lord, we intercede;
  Make thou our sad divisions soon to cease;
Draw us the nearer each to each, we plead,
  By drawing all to thee, O Prince of Peace;
Thus may we all one bread, one body be,
Through this blest sacrament of unity.

So, Lord, at length when sacraments shall cease,
  May we be one with all thy church above,
One with thy saints in one unbroken peace,
  One with thy saints in one unbounded love;
More blessèd still, in peace and love to be
One with the Trinity in unity.

                                        W. H. Turton

322   *From SANCTUARY*

Around Christ's table we commune,
  In fellowship supreme;
Inspired by Christ, through word and tune,
  Of things divine we dream.

Forth from this sacred place we go,
  With challenge in each soul,
To love, to lift, to build, to grow,
  God's Kingdom is our goal.

                                     Harold L. Humbert

323   *A GENERAL COMMUNION*

I saw the throng, so deeply separate,
  Fed at one only board—
The devout people, moved, intent, elate,
  And the devoted Lord.

O struck apart! not side from human side,
  But soul from human soul,
As each asunder absorbed and multiplied,
  The ever unparted, whole.

I saw this people as a field of flowers,
   Each grown at such a price
The sum of unimaginable powers
   Did no more than suffice.

A thousand single central daisies they,
   A thousand of the one;
For each, the entire monopoly of day;
   For each, the whole of the devoted sun.

Alice Meynell

324   *MEDITATION FOR HOLY COMMUNION*

Thy love, O Christ, requires a fellowship
With creatures made in image like to thine,
Though they be full of sin, not so divine
Of nature, or of life, to merit sip
From sacred chalice, or to bring to lip
The bread. Yet out of love thou didst resign
Thyself to death in order to refine
Man's dross. What to thee the thorns and whip,
Ridicule, betrayal and denial?
Thou, matchless Christ, wert true to man and God.
Thy love and spirit now put us on trial;
We stand condemned unless we live to laud.
O Christ, implant thy spirit now in me
That I may live in fellowship with thee.

Russell Q. Chilcote

325   *WHOSO SUFFERS MOST*

"I am the True Vine," said our Lord, "and ye,
My brethren, are the branches." And that Vine,
Then first uplifted in its place, and hung
With its first purple grapes, since then has grown,
Until its green leaves gladden half the world,
And from its countless clusters rivers flow
For healing of the nations, and its boughs
Innumerable strength through all the earth,
Ever increasing, ever each entwined

With each, all living from the Central Heart.
And you and I, my brethren, live and grow,
Branches of that immortal human Stem.

Measure thy life by loss instead of gain;
Not by the wine drunk, but the wine poured forth;
For love's strength standeth in love's sacrifice;
And whoso suffers most hath most to give.

Harriet Eleanor King

326   *From THE VISION OF SIR LAUNFAL*

As Sir Launfal mused with a downcast face,
A light shone round about the place;
The leper no longer crouched at his side,
But stood before him glorified,
Shining and tall and fair and straight
As the pillar that stood by the Beautiful Gate,—
Himself the Gate whereby men can
Enter the temple of God in Man.

His words were shed softer than leaves from the pine,
And they fell on Sir Launfal as snows on the brine,
That mingle their softness and quiet in one
With the shaggy unrest their float down upon;
And the voice that was softer than silence said,
"Lo it is I, be not afraid!
In many climes, without avail,
Thou hast spent thy life for the Holy Grail;
Behold, it is here,—this cup which thou
Didst fill at the streamlet for me but now;
This crust is my body broken for thee,
This water his blood that died on the tree;
The Holy Supper is kept, indeed,
In whatso we share with another's need;
Not what we give, but what we share,
For the gift without the giver is bare;
Who gives himself with his alms feeds three,
Himself, his hungering neighbor, and me."

James Russell Lowell

327   *MY PART*

> Memorials, signs, and seals of grace—
>   And channels too—I see:
> Nor would I fail the part to trace
>   This service puts on *me;*
> With all thy members I commune—
>   Thy death show forth to men—
> And, grateful for the covenant-boon,
>   Subscribe the bond again.

W. M. Bunting

328   *BENEATH THE FORMS OF OUTWARD RITE*

> Beneath the forms of outward rite
> Thy supper, Lord, is spread
> In every quiet upper room
> Where fainting souls are fed.
>
> The bread is always consecrate
> Which men divide with men;
> And every act of brotherhood
> Repeats thy feast again.
>
> The blessed cup is only passed
> True memory of thee,
> When life anew pours out its wine
> With rich sufficiency.
>
> O Master, through these symbols shared,
> Thine own dear self impart,
> That in our daily life may flame
> The passion of thy heart.

James A. Blaisdell

329   *COME, HOLY GHOST*

Come, Holy Ghost, thine influence shed,
  And realize[1] the sign;
Thy life infuse into the bread,
  Thy power into the wine.
Effectual let the tokens prove,
  And made, by heavenly art,
Fit channels to convey thy love
  To every faithful heart.

Charles Wesley

[1] make real

330   *SACRAMENT*

There lies no magic in this bit of bread,
  No charm to save me in this sip of wine.
No food can nourish if the soul be dead,
  No lifeless heart respond to fire divine.

Here at God's altar I may kneel in vain
  Unless I glow with love, selfless and deep.
When I do truly serve my fellow men
  The eucharist I keep.

Una W. Harsen

331   *THE EUCHARIST*

Whene'er I seek the holy altar's rail,
  And kneel to take the grace there offered me,
It is no time to task my reason frail,
  To try Christ's words, and search how they may be;
Enough, I eat his flesh and drink his blood,
More is not told—to ask it is not good.

I will not say with these, that bread and wine
  Have vanished at the consecration prayer;
Far less with those deny that aught divine
  And of immortal seed is hidden there.

Hence, disputants! The din, which ye admire,
Keeps but ill measure with the church's choir.

John Henry Newman

332   *OLDEST DEACON*

We saw him at the altar, waiting there
To pass the bread and wine in memory.
At times the sun's soft fingers touched his hair—
A frosted crown above serenity
Of face, assured by secrets hid from us,
After the furious beatings of life's ways,
Where thoughts seem neither glad nor ominous,
So near a world that counts not time by days.

So near, and yet with time to look afar,
Beyond horizons we may not define,
Hurried and troubled, restless as we are—
But when we saw that old man pass the wine,
Through quietude a still voice seemed to say:
"Be not dismayed. The stone is rolled away."

Ida Norton Munson

333   *AFTER COMMUNION*

Why should I call thee Lord, who are my God?
    Why should I call thee Friend, who art my love?
    Or King, who art my very spouse above?
Or call thy sceptre on my heart thy rod?
    Lo now thy banner over me is love,
All heaven flies open to me at thy nod:
For thou hast lit thy flame in me a clod,
    Made me a nest for dwelling of thy dove.
    What wilt thou call me in our home above,
Who now hast called me friend? how will it be
        When thou for good wine settest forth the best?
Now thou dost bid me come and sup with thee,
        Now thou dost make me lean upon thy breast:
    How will it be with me in time of love?

Christina G. Rossetti

334   *COMMUNION HYMN OF NOVALIS*

Never endeth that sweet meal,
Love doth never take its fill.
Hungrier and thirstier
Grows the heart;
And so love's pleasure lasts
Through all eternity.

Index of Texts

INDEX OF TEXTS

REFERENCES ARE TO ITEM NUMBERS

Genesis 28:16 212
Exodus 24:4-8 181
1 Chronicles 16:11 235
Psalm 2:5 116
    116:12 116
    116:13 116
    118:1 252
    118:17 252
    118:22-23 252
    118:26 252
    118:28-29 252
Proverbs 23:7 173
Jeremiah 31:31 181
Matthew 11:29 116
    14:19 162
    18:20 136
    20:22 182
    26:7 242
    26:18-20 132
    26:22 245
    26:25 242
    26:26 114
    26:27-28 183
    26:28 116
    26:30 248, 249
Mark 8:31 252
    10:39 182
    11:9-10 252
    14:18 246
    14:24 117, 182
    14:24-25 232
    14:25 234
    14:50 246

Luke 2:25 116
    14:18 116
    22:10 123
    22:15 125
    22:19 116
    22:19-20 188
    22:20 116, 117, 181
    22:28 128, 129
    22:48 241
    24:30-31 169
    24:31 116, 166
    24:33 170
John 6:27 116
    6:33 140
    6:34 116
    6:53 120, 147
    6:56 116, 147
    11:56 135
    12:36 179
    13:3 237
    13:5 237
    13:27 245
    13:35 116
    15:5 240
    15:7 176
    17:23 116
    20:21 114
Acts 2:1 200
    2:42 116, 166, 200, 201
    2:46 168
Romans 5:8 192
    11:33 116
    12:5 217

1 Corinthians 1:9   201
    5:7   116
    10:16   201
    10:16-17   206
    11:23   107, 168, 198, 224,
       244
    11:24   190
    11:25   114
    11:26   106, 116, 192, 234
    11:28   263, 265
    11:29   269
    11:31   269
    12:13   116
    16:1   116
2 Corinthians 1:22   116
    6:14   201
    7:9   116
    13:14   201

Ephesians 3:2   116
    3:9   201
Philippians 1:5   201
    1:6   159
    2:1   201
    3:10   201
Colossians 1:24   197
    2:14   116
2 Timothy 1:14   196
    2:12   196
Hebrews 9:14   116
    13:9   116
1 Peter 1:11   233
    2:24   116
    4:1   116
    5:5   116
1 John 1:3   201
    1:6   201
Revelation 2:25   114

Index of Poetry

INDEX OF POETRY

REFERENCES ARE TO ITEM NUMBERS

Titles are listed in italics to distinguish them from first line references.

According to thy gracious word 277

After Communion 333

Alas, my God, that we should be 292

All praise to him of Nazareth 273

Amidst us our Beloved stands 271

And could'st thou, Lord, thy thanks express 278

And have the bright immensities 288

And so we come; O draw us to thy feet 303

AQUINAS, THOMAS 300

Around Christ's table we commune 322

As Sir Launfal mused with a downcast face 326

At many an altar I have knelt 294

BAKER, HENRY W. 298

Beneath the forms of outward rite 328

BERNARD OF CLAIRVAUX 312

BICKERSTHETH, EDWARD HENRY 290, 328

BLAISDELL, JAMES A. 328

BONAR, HORATIUS 299, 320

BRADBY, GODFREY FOX 282

Bread 315

Bread of the world in mercy broken 314

Break thou the bread of life 313

BRIGHT, WILLIAM 303

BROWNLIE, JOHN 316

BRYANT, WILLIAM CULLEN 273

BUNTING, W. M. 327

BYROM, JOHN 295

CHILCOTE, RUSSELL Q. 324

CLARK, LESLIE SAVAGE 276, 315

Come, Holy Ghost, thine influence shed 329

Come ye yourselves apart and rest awhile 290

Communion (extract) (Bonar) 320

Communion (Slater) 307

Communion Hymn of Novalis 334

COWPER, WILLIAM 296

CROWELL, GRACE NOLL 294

CUSHMAN, RALPH SPAULDING 279

Deck thyself, my soul, with gladness 304

Desponding Soul's Wish, The 295

Dim tracts of time divide 272

Do This 282

Each meal should be a sacramental feast 319

Emmaus 286

Eucharist, The 331

FORD, CHARLES L. 274
FROTHINGHAM, NATHANIEL
           LANGDON 275

General Communion, A 323
GRANT, WILLIAM 278

HARKNESS, GEORGIA 291
HARSEN, UNA W. 330
He is my Altar; I, his holy Place
     317
He knew what hunger a man can
     feel 315
HEBER, REGINALD 314
HERBERT, GEORGE 293
Here, O my Lord, I see thee face to
     face 299
HOSMER, FREDERICK L. 289
HOUSMAN, LAURENCE 286
How happy are thy servants, Lord
     301
HUMBERT, HAROLD F. 322

"I am the True Vine," said our
     Lord, "and ye 325
I give my body for your sake 282
I saw the throng, so deeply separate
     323
If in the press of every day 291
Invitation, The 290
It was no enemy which did this
     wrong 280

JACOBS, HENRY E. 311
Jesus, Thou Joy of Loving Hearts
     (extract) 312

KING, HARRIET ELEANOR
     325
King of Love, The (extract) 298

Last Supper, The 283
LATHBURY, MARY A. 313
Let thy blood in mercy poured
     316
Love 293

Love bade me welcome; yet my
     soul drew back 293
LOWELL, JAMES RUSSELL
     326

Man of Nazareth, The (extract)
     289
Meditation for Holy Communion
     324
Memorials, signs, and seals of grace
     327
MEYNELL, ALICE 323
MILLER, JOAQUIN 283
MONTGOMERY, JAMES 277
MORLEY, FREDERICK B. 302
MORRISON, JOHN 281
MUNSON, IDA NORTON 285,
     332
My Beloved Is Mine (extract) 317
My broken body thus I give 281
My Part 327
My spirit longeth for thee 295

Never endeth that sweet meal 334
NEWMAN, JOHN HENRY 331
Not worthy, Lord, to gather up the
     crumbs 306

O bread to pilgrims given 309
O Friend and Brother, draw more
     near 289
O thou who this mysterious bread
     287
Oh heart, be humble and adore
     307
Oldest Deacon 332
One Christ we feed upon, one living
     Christ 320
OXENHAM, JOHN 297, 319

PALGRAVE, FRANCIS
     TURNER 272
POTEAT, EDWIN McNEILL
     284

Prayer for the Presence of Christ, A   310

QUARLES, FRANCIS   317
Quest, The   291

"Remember me," the Saviour said   275
Remembrance   276
Reveal thy presence now, O Lord   310
Road to Emmaus, The   285
ROBBINS, HOWARD CHANDLER   288
ROBERTSON, W. G.   318
ROSSETTI, CHRISTINA G.   333

Sacrament (Crowell)   294
Sacrament, The (Ford)   274
Sacrament (Harsen)   330
Sacrament, The (Wells)   308
Sacrament of Food, The   319
Sanctuary (extract)   322
SHEPHERD, THOMAS   292
SLATER, ELEANOR   307
Sop, The   280
Spread Table, The   297
SPURGEON, CHARLES H.   271

Table Triplets   318
That They All May Be One   321
The sun lay warm on tawny fields   276
The symbols of thy sacrament   308
Thee we adore, O hidden Saviour, thee   300
There lies no magic in this bit of bread   330
There was a chalice in the ancient East   284
They, with a stranger, broke the bread   286
This Do in Remembrance of Me (extract)   299
"This is my body, which is given for you"   274

This is the feast of heavenly wine   296
Thou spread'st a table in my sight   298
Thou who, at thy first eucharist, didst pray   321
Thy love, O Christ, requires a fellowship   324
TIPLADY, THOMAS   310
To thee I come, thou gracious Christ   302
TURTON, W. H.   321
Twilight. And on a dusty ribboned road   285
Two Chalices   284

Upper Room Communion Hymn   302

Via Lucis   288
Vision of Sir Launfel, The (extract)   326

We saw him at the altar, waiting there   332
We taste thee, O thou living Bread   312
Welcome to the Table   296
WELLS, AMOS R.   308
WESLEY, CHARLES   287, 301, 329
What he did at supper seated   305
What song sang the twelve with the Saviour   283
What were his thoughts   279
When Jesus Washed the Feet of Judas (extract)   279
When'er I seek the holy altar's rail   331
Where'er I be, Lord, spread for me   297
Whoso Suffers Most   325
Why should I call thee Lord, who art my God   333

Year by year, the Man Divine   318

Index of Days and Seasons

INDEX OF DAYS AND SEASONS

The small letters in parentheses preceding item numbers identify calls to worship and opening scriptural sentences by c, invocations and opening prayers by i, litanies and responsive prayers by l, affirmations and confessions by a, prayers by p, homiletical quotations and resources by q, and poems and verse quotations by v.

Advent—(c) 12, 14, 17-19, 21, 22, 24; (i) 34; (p) 50, 53, 54; (q) 106, 135, 137, 235, 270; (v) 273, 288, 292

All Saints' Day—(c) 11, 16, 19; (i) 32; (l) 85; (p) 48, 50, 52, 69, 82, 83; (q) 110, 202, 210, 212, 218; (v) 321

Ascension Sunday—(c) 11; (p) 67; (q) 166, 168, 233; (v) 288, 289, 304

Baptism, service of—(c) 14, 16, 20, 21, 24; (i) 34; (p) 52, 60, 69; (a) 100; (q) 157, 159, 180, 188, 223, 224, 240; (v) 316

Bible Sunday—(c) 20, 23; (i) 26; (a) 96, 97; (q) 107, 110, 114, 123, 146, 157, 193, 194, 239

Brotherhood Sunday—(c) 14; (i) 31-33; (p) 50, 56, 83; (l) 85; (a) 102; (q) 127, 139, 145, 170, 200, 207, 208, 210, 216, 217, 225, 228, 236, 247, 256; (v) 301, 311, 324, 326, 328

Christmas—(c) 17, 23; (p) 66; (q) 107, 121, 176

Church anniversary and dedication —(c) 20, 25; (p) 56; (l) 89-91; (q) 117, 123, 167, 176, 186, 194, 202, 206, 207, 213, 215, 216, 218; (v) 321

Easter—(i) 30, 33; (l) 88; (q) 112, 134, 169-171, 177, 188; (v) 273, 285-288, 318, 332

Good Friday—(c) 10; (i) 28; (p) 48, 51, 52, 55, 66, 74, 75; (q) 114, 130, 139, 147, 175, 177, 181-186, 190, 192, 206, 212, 244, 252, 255; (v) 281, 282

Home, festival of the Christian— (c) 15; (i) 32; (p) 76; (l) 85; (q) 105, 159, 230; (v) 319

Independence Sunday—(q) 208, 221, 222

Labor Sunday—(i) 27; (p) 78; (q) 145, 151; (v) 294

Lent—(c) 10, 20, 22, 24; (i) 27, 28, 33, 35; (p) 48, 51, 53, 58, 78, 82; (q) 130, 131, 133, 136, 137, 143, 158, 174, 178, 180, 184, 190, 196, 197, 238, 244, 262, 266; (v) 290, 291, 293, 295, 306, 315

Maundy Thursday—(c) 10; (i) 35; (p) 48, 51-56, 58, 59, 62, 71, 73-75; (q) 109, 114, 124-133, 166, 167, 179, 211, 231, 241-252; (v) 274, 275, 279, 280, 283

Missionary Sunday—(c) 18; (i) 32; (p) 50, 56, 57, 83; (l) 89, 90; (a) 98; (q) 109, 112, 170, 195, 198, 223-225, 236; (v) 330

New members, reception of—(c) 16; (i) 27); (p) 52, 60; (a) 100; (q) 104, 128, 129, 133, 161, 180, 190, 196, 240; (v) 316

New Year Sunday—(c) 20, 21, 24; (i) 26, 35; (p) 63, 77, 81; (q) 172, 197, 234; (v) 290, 291

Pentecost—(c) 19; (i) 30, 35; (p) 68, 80, 83; (l) 89-91; (a) 98; (q) 109, 123, 139, 167, 178, 186, 200, 206, 207, 213, 215, 216, 228; (v) 321, 329

Prayer, week of—(c) 24; (p) 59; (q) 108, 133, 200, 219, 247

Reformation Sunday—(c) 21; (p) 49; (q) 159, 209, 217, 253-258

Rural Life Sunday—(p) 84; (q) 144, 145, 151, 155, 156, 176; (v) 276, 318

Stewardship Sunday—(c) 21; (i) 30, 32; (q) 133, 151, 186, 196, 200, 201, 219, 237, 242; (v) 326, 327, 330

Thanksgiving Sunday—(c) 21, 23; (i) 31, 32; (p) 67, 84; (l) 91; (q) 111, 112, 117, 162, 221; (v) 278

Washington's Birthday—(q) 222

World Communion Sunday—(c) 14, 15; (i) 31; (p) 50, 56, 57, 76, 83; (l) 85, 90, 91; (q) 109, 110, 117, 122, 139, 171, 200, 202, 206-217, 228, 256; (v) 301, 311, 321

Index of Authors and Sources

INDEX OF AUTHORS AND SOURCES

NAMES OF AUTHORS AND BOOK TITLES ARE LISTED BY ITEM NUMBERS

Acts of Devotion 80

Adamson, Robert M.—*The Christian Doctrine of the Lord's Supper* 165

Alexander, James W.—*Sacramental Discourses* 249

Andrewes, Lancelot—*The Private Devotions of* 116

Arndt, Elmer J. F.—*The Heritage of the Reformation* 134, 193, 202

Arseniev, Nicholas—*Mysticism and the Eastern Church* 213

Atkinson, Lowell M. 58, 59

Austin, John 37

Babcock, Maltbie D.—*Thoughts for Every-Day Living* 77

Bader, Jesse M.—*Communion Meditations* 200

Barclay, William—*A New Testament Wordbook* 201

Barnes-Lawrence, Arthur Evelyn—*The Holy Communion* 215

Beeching, H. C.—*The Bible Doctrine of the Sacraments* 269

Bell, Robert B. H. 36

Bethune, Roderick—*The Sacramental Table* 172

Black, Hugh—*Christ's Service of Love* 196, 263

Blackwood, Andrew W.—*The Fine*

Art of Public Worship 230

Book of Common Worship, The 8

Book of Family Worship, A 74

Bowie, Walter Russell—*Lift Up Your Hearts* 73, 99

Brilioth, Yngve—*Eucharistic Faith and Practice* 107

Brooke, Stopford A.—*The Kingship of Love* 187

Brown, Robert McAfee—*The Significance of the Church* 110

Bruce, Alexander Balmain—*The Training of the Twelve* 138, 184

Brunner, Emil—*The Great Invitation* 206; *Our Faith* 123

Budge, Ronald H. G.—*The Sacramental Table* 67

Bunyan, John—*The Pilgrim's Progress* 205

Burnaby, John—*Christian Words and Christian Meanings* 240

Burnet, Adam W.—*The Sacramental Table* 239

Buttrick, George A.—*Prayer* 85, 108

Calvin, John—*Institutes of the Christian Religion* 255, 256

Cameron, Hugh—*Prayers for Use in Public Worship* 27

Carey, S. Pearce—*William Carey* 223

Christian-Evangelist, The 222

Chrysostom 66

Coffin, Henry Sloane 236

Craig, Clarence Tucker—*The Beginnings of Christianity* 168; *Man's Disorder and God's Design* 207

Crane, Henry Hitt—*Communion Meditations* 173

Crothers, Samuel M.—*Prayers* 49

Dawson, George—*Prayers* 47, 84

Devotional Offices for General Use 88

Dibelius, Martin—*Jesus* 167

Dodd, C. H.—*The Apostolic Preaching* 177; *Christian Worship* 233

Drury, S. S.—*Draw Near with Faith* 121

Edwards, Jonathan—*An Humble Inquiry* 180

Faichney, T. T.—*Upper Room Pulpit* 195

Fairbairn, A. M.—*Studies in the Life of Christ* 214

Falconer, P. J. Bisset—*The Sacramental Table* 48

Family Devotions 78

Farmer, Herbert H.—*The Healing Cross* 190

Fey, Harold E.—*The Lord's Supper* 176, 209

Finegan, Jack—*Book of Student Prayers* 55

Fiske, Charles—*The Christ We Know* 175; *The Master's Memorial* 53

Fosdick, Harry Emerson—*On Being Fit to Live With* 128

Freeman, Elmer S.—*The Lord's Supper in Protestantism* 111

Gladden, Washington—*How Much Is Left of the Old Doctrines?* 143, 174

Gore, Charles—*The Body of Christ* 186

Gossip, Arthur John—*Experience Worketh Hope* 124, 194

Guhsé, H. P.—*A Book of Invocations* 26

Halverson, Marvin P.—*Religious Symbolism* 253

Harris, Thomas L.—*Christian Public Worship* 5

Hunt, George Laird—*Rediscovering the Church* 259

Hunter, John—*Devotional Services* 28, 34, 51

Hutchison, Owen—*Christian Love in Everyday Living* 210

Hutton, John A.—*There They Crucified Him* 118, 237, 250

Hyde, William DeWitt—*Outlines in Social Theology* 189

Hymns of the United Church 92

Inge, William R. 185; *Personal Religion and the Life of Devotion* 164

Intercession Services 89

Jansen, John Frederick—*Guests of God* 159

Jenkins, Daniel—*Tradition, Freedom and the Spirit* 106

Jeremias, Joachim—*The Eucharistic Words of Jesus* 252

Johnson, Samuel—*The Prayers of* 75

Jones, E. Stanley—*The Christ of Every Road* 131

Jowett, John Henry—*The Friend on the Road* 198, 241; *The Whole Armour of God* 54

Kay, J. Alan—*The Nature of Christian Worship* 191

Kean, Charles Duell—*Making Sense Out of Life* 151

Keighton, Robert E.—*Minister's Communion Service Book* 71

Kierkegaard, Søren—*Christian Discourses* 244

Kingsley, Charles 203; *Village Sermons* 264

Knox, John—*The Manner of the Lord's Supper* 254

Lambert, John C.—*The Sacraments of the New Testament* 146

Large, John E.—*Lift Up Your Hearts* 270

Laymon, Charles M.—*The Life and Teachings of Jesus* 245

Levens, J. T.—*Aspects of the Holy Communion* 112, 122, 208

Lilley, J. P.—*The Lord's Supper* 137

Lilley, Philip W.—*The Sacramental Table* 183

Lindsay, Thomas M.—*A History of the Reformation* 258

Liturgy of Malabar 79

Liturgy of St. James 30

Liturgy of St. Mark 68, 83

London Yearly Meeting 204

Lowrie, Walter—*The Short Story of Jesus* 234

Luccock, Robert E.—*If God Be for Us* 218

Mabie, Hamilton Wright—*Fruits of the Spirit* 133

Maclagen, P. J.—*The Gospel and Its Working* 225

Maclaren, Alexander—*Pulpit Prayers* 87

Maclean, Norman—*Communion Addresses* 212

MacLennan, David A.—*Joyous Adventure* 76

McKee, Elmore McNeill—*Communion with God* 56

Manson, William—*Luke (Moffatt New Testament Commentary)* 181

Martineau, James—*Home Prayers* 81; *Hours of Thought on Sacred Things* 266

Martyr, Justin—*First Apology* 219

Mascall, E. L.—*Christ, the Christian and the Church* 145

Matheson, George—*Studies of the Portrait of Christ* 125

Mathews, Basil—*A Life of Jesus* 127

Maurice, Frederick Denison—*The Eucharist* 267

Maxwell, William D.—*An Outline of Christian Worship* 257

Menzies, Robert—*Fight the Good Fight* 226

Micklem, Nathaniel—*Christian Worship* 114; *Ultimate Questions* 160

Miller, Samuel H.—*The Great Realities* 152; *Prayers for Daily Use* 4, 72

Minister's Book of Prayers, The 60

Morgan, G. Campbell—*Searchlights from the Word* 248, 265

Morrison, Charles Clayton—*What Is Christianity?* 211

Morrison, George H.—*Communion Addresses* 135; *Sun-Rise* 149; *The Weaving of Glory* 163, 169

Morrison, James Dalton—*Minister's Service Book* 1, 33; *The New Church Hymnal* 86

Moule, Handley C. G. 136

Nash, H. S. 31

National Council of Churches 57

Neill, Stephen—*The Christian Society* 119, 199

Newbigin, Lesslie—*The Household of God* 188

Newman, John Henry—*Parochial and Plain Sermons, VII* 235

Newton, Joseph Fort—*Altar Stairs* 50

Niemöller, Martin—*Dachau Sermons* 228

Osborn, G. Edwin—*Christian Worship* 6

Palmer, Albert W.—*The Art of Conducting Public Worship* 3

Parker, Joseph—*The Inner Life of Jesus* 120, 162

Paton, John G.—*Autobiography* 224

Peabody, Francis Greenwood—*Mornings in the College Chapel* 150

Ramsay, R. Guy—*The Sacramental Table* 192

Rauschenbusch, Walter—*Prayers of the Social Awakening* 32, 100

Rees, Edward Jeffries—*In Remembrance of Me* 247, 262

Reinhard, V. R. 82

Roberts, Richard 101; *The Spirit of God and the Faith of Man* 129; *That One Face* 260

Robertson, Frederick W.—*Sermons* 156

Robertston, James A.—*The Spiritual Pilgrimage of Jesus* 182

Robinson, W.—*A Companion to the Communion Service* 105

Rowley, H. H.—*The Unity of the Bible* 117

Sardeson, Charles T.—*Rediscovering the Words of Faith* 157

Scherer, Paul—*Facts That Undergird Life* 130

Schlink, Edmund—*Man's Disorder and God's Design* 229

Sclater, J. R. P.—*The Public Worship of God* 144

Scott, Ernest F.—*The Nature of the Early Church* 166

Scriver, Christian 142

Services of Religion 35

Simpson, P. Carnegie—*The Fact of the Christian Church* 161

Slattery, Charles Lewis 139; *The Master's Memorial* 62

Smith, David—*The Pilgrim's Hospice* 69, 231

Smith, John—*The Generall Historie of Virginia* 221

Sockman, Ralph W.—*How to Believe* 141

Spurgeon, Charles H.—*Great Pulpit Masters, II* 217, 251

Stalker, James—*Life of Christ* 126

Stamm, Frederick Keller—*The Conversations of Jesus* 238

Stewart, George—*Jesus Said I Am* 261

Stewart, James S.—*The Strong Name* 132

Stoffel, Ernest Lee—*His Kingdom Is Forever* 232

Strayer, Paul Moore—*A Sheaf of Prayers* 52

Studdert-Kennedy, G. A.—*The Best of* 148

Taylor, Jeremy—*Works* 268

Temple, William—*Christ the Truth* 154, 197; *Readings in St. John's Gospel* 147

Thomas, David Owen—*At the Lord's Table* 170, 179

Tiplady, Thomas—*The Cross at the Front* 227

Tittle, Ernest Fremont—*The Gospel According to Luke* 104

Tolstoy, Leo 102

Underhill, Evelyn—*Worship* 178

Vance, James I.—*The Master's Memorial* 242

Wagner, Hughes—*The Word in Season* 103

Walker, Harold Blake—*Power to Manage Yourself* 246

Watson, John—*The Mind of the Master* 216

Weatherhead, Leslie D.—*The Transforming Friendship* 140

Wesley, John—*Journal of* 115

Whale, J. S.—*What Is a Living Church?* 113

Wolf, William J.—*Man's Knowledge of God* 171

World Council of Churches 90, 91

Wotherspoon, H. J.—*Religious Values in the Sacraments* 153, 158

Wright, C. J.—*The Mission and Message of Jesus* 155, 243

Wyon, Olive—*The Altar Fire* 109, 220

Index of Subjects

INDEX OF SUBJECTS

REFERENCES ARE TO ITEM NUMBERS

adoration, action and 195
atonement, doctrine of 184, 206
Augustine 256

baptism 123, 157, 159, 207, 223, 224
    of Christ 188
Barth, Karl 226
benediction 153
Bethany, anointing at 125, 242
Bible, interpreting of 123
body, spirit and 148
Body of Christ, church as 114, 117, 171, 206
bread 120, 143-151, 189, 206, 315
Bread, Christ as the 138, 140, 274, 296, 312, 314
"breaking of bread" 168, 170, 313, 319
Bridegroom, Christ as the 271
Brooks, Phillips 270
brotherhood, Christian 127, 139, 170, 256, 328

Calvin, John 253
Carey, William 223
charity 294
Christ Jesus, abiding in 148, 240
    absence of 135
    adoration of 300, 309
    anointing of 125, 242
    appeal of 236
    ascension of 289
    baptism of 188

Christ Jesus—*Continued*
    betrayal of 241, 242, 244-246, 274, 280
    as Bread of Life 138, 140, 274, 296, 312, 314
    as the Bridegroom 271
    centrality of 148, 176, 194, 260
    coming of 106, 135, 148, 194, 235, 270, 292, 307
    commitment to 180, 196, 297, 316, 319
    communion with 117, 125, 135, 140, 258, 287, 292, 297
    as Companion 169, 171, 285
    confidence in 196
    contact with 158
    as Contemporary 141
    death of 117, 175, 181, 183, 184, 212, 229, 239, 273, 278, 314, 324
    desire of 125
    exaltation of 126
    example of 256
    face of 261
    family of 127
    feeding upon 114, 120, 138, 140, 180, 287, 302, 311, 312
    fellowship with 134, 135, 143, 167, 201, 217, 257, 265, 289, 324
    fidelity to 223

Christ Jesus—*Continued*
  following 272
  forgetting 172
  friendship of 126, 140, 142, 333
  grace of 314
  as Guest 295
  hidden 300
  incarnation of 107
  indwelling 110, 306
  invitation of 290, 293, 296, 303, 306, 333
  joy of 251
  as King 138, 220
  love of 126, 183, 240, 243, 245, 273, 278, 281, 293, 307, 324, 333
  love toward 165, 256
  misunderstanding of 128
  obedience of 182
  oneness in 117, 127, 134, 208, 256
  parables of 146
  partaking of 143, 213
  partnership with 201
  as Paschal Lamb 184, 274
  passion of 248
  personal 158, 173
  personality of 143, 169
  preparing way of 270
  presence of 114, 124, 134-137, 139, 141, 166, 170, 178, 197, 204, 271, 286, 288, 297, 300, 310
  as Priest 138, 319
  as Prophet 138
  receiving of 154
  recognition of 170, 271, 287
  redemption of 181, 184
  rejection of 243
  remembering of 121, 123, 130, 166, 172-176, 188, 220, 234, 273, 275-277, 282, 286, 302

Christ Jesus—*Continued*
  resurrection of 131, 188, 273, 288, 318
  return of 168, 229, 234, 235, 289
  return to 266
  sacramental teaching of 155
  sacrifice of 154, 175, 178, 181-185, 258, 314
  sacrificial love of 189
  self-giving of 139, 142, 154, 243, 282, 316
  selflessness of 264
  as Servant 236-239
  serving 242
  simplicity of 149
  as Singing-master 251
  table of 136, 139, 322
  triumph of 119
  as the Truth 244
  unity in 206, 211, 216, 228, 233, 256, 301, 311
  as the Vine 119, 176, 240, 325
  welcome of 293, 296, 333
  will of 321
  as the Word 313
  yearning for 312
Christian brotherhood 127, 139, 170, 256, 328
Christian community 207
Christian fellowship 110, 199-202, 204, 208, 209, 212, 217, 257, 322, 324
Christian friendship 201
Christian harmony 247, 301
Christian love 210, 216, 225, 240
Christian society 216
Christian "togetherness" 207
Christian unity 200, 209, 211, 212, 216, 228, 256, 301, 311, 321

Christianity, validation of 122
church, as Body of Christ 114, 117, 171, 206
buttress of 123
communion with 117, 218
divisions in 321, 331
early 108, 119, 157, 199, 200, 219, 230
foundation of 167
sacraments and 207
sacrifice of 186
unity of 206, 207, 212, 216, 228, 321
collection 219
common things 110, 151
confession 111
communion, with Christ 117, 125, 135, 140, 258, 287, 292, 297
with the church 117, 218
with God 107, 113
of saints 110, 210, 321
spiritual 107
cooperation 145
covenant, Lord's Supper as 117, 127, 179-182, 281
cross, challenge of the 190, 282
as symbol 153, 155
cup, communion 182, 260, 284, 326, 328 [see Holy Grail]
Passover 127

deacon 332
democracy, of Lord's Supper 208
disciples 106, 114, 125-130, 166, 167, 188, 211, 216, 231, 246, 283
discipleship 220, 240
Drake, Francis 172
"dry communion" 253

early church 108, 119, 157, 199, 200, 219, 230
ekklesia 207
Emerson, Ralph Waldo 141

Emmaus, journey to 166, 169-171, 285-287
enemy 225, 226
Erskine, Ebenezer 212
eternal life 147
eucharist, Lord's Supper as 107, 109, 112, 117, 119, 331
evil, deceptiveness of 241
expectancy, spirit of 172

faith 110, 113, 200
family, of Christ 127
family meal, Lord's Supper as 230
fear 131
feeding of the multitude 162, 313, 315
fellowship, of believers 210
with Christ 134, 135, 143, 167, 201, 217, 257, 265, 289, 324
Christian 110, 199-202, 204, 208, 209, 212, 217, 257, 322, 324
of faith 200
with God 113, 201
Lord's Supper as 117, 165, 167, 199, 200, 202, 217
of love 200
of prayer 200
in the Spirit 201
table 167, 168, 171
"fellowship in holy things" 207
food, as sacrament 319
footwashing, of disciples 126, 236-240, 279, 280
forgiveness, of sin 111, 175, 183, 225, 296, 302, 314
friendship 140
of Christ 126, 140, 142, 333
Christian 201

generosity 326
God, action of 185, 191, 193-195
communion with 107, 113

God—*Continued*
 fellowship with   113, 201
 forgiveness of   175
 grace of   155
 guest of   162
 love of   139, 187, 210
 need of   133
 presence of   204
 purpose of   319
 simplicity of   149
 union with   147
Goethe, Johann Wolfgang von
  192
Gospel, enactment of   110
grace, covenant of   180

Hallēl   248, 252
heart, burning   170
 enlarged   120
Holy Grail   284, 291, 326
Holy Spirit   201, 207, 292, 329
humility   302
hunger   315
hymn, of Upper Room   248-252,
  283

insignificant, revelation of   169

Jamestown, Virginia   221
John (disciple)   220, 283
John (gospel)   117, 239, 240
joy, of Christ   251
 of Lord's Supper   112, 232,
  304
Judas   238, 241-247, 279, 280

king, Christ as   138, 220
Kingdom of God   177, 322
kiss, of betrayal   241, 244
koinōnia   110, 201

labor   151, 294
life, sacramental   159, 162, 164
 sacredness of   110
 significance of   110

Lincoln, Abraham   141
Lord's Supper, as action of God
  185, 191, 193-195
 appeal of   103, 108, 229
 aspects of   105, 113, 116,
  138, 139, 181
 attendance at   199, 222
 benefits of   256, 322
 blessings of   308
 centrality of   109, 253, 257
 collection at   219
 continuity of   106, 109, 122,
  214, 215, 220, 275, 328,
  334
 as covenant   117, 127, 179-
  182, 281
 as democratic rite   208
 eschatological element of   119
  [*see* messianic banquet]
 eternal aspect of   113
 exclusion from   199, 217
 as family meal   230
 as fellowship   117, 165, 167,
  199, 200, 202, 217
 as festival of hope   231
 historical witness of   122,
  219, 253, 258
 hymn at   248-252, 283
 instituting of   123, 126, 127,
  138, 184, 188, 189
 invitation to   290, 293, 296,
  303
 joy of   112, 232, 304
 meaning of   109, 114, 115,
  117, 118, 121, 159, 183,
  191
 as memorial   113, 121, 234,
  305 [*see* Christ, remembering of]
 message of   231
 misuse of   239, 269
 neglect of   123, 253
 obligation of   327
 origins of   166, 167

Lord's Supper—*Continued*
    as a parable 146
    perspectives of 114
    preparation for 111, 115, 203, 263-268, 270
    promise of 308
    purpose of 118, 123, 143, 189, 206, 254, 256
    relevance of 132
    as a sacrament 117 [*see* sacraments]
    sacrificial character of 181-186, 258
    service of 219, 253
    significance of 117, 123, 178, 214, 259
    simplicity of 149, 171
    social significance of 117
    speculation concerning 119
    as spiritual drama 192
    symbolism of 104, 108, 143, 144, 146, 149, 154
    as thanksgiving 111, 112, 114, 117
    universality of 122, 139, 145, 209, 214, 215, 228
    worship and 108, 109, 111
love, fellowship of 200
    of Christ 126, 183, 240, 243, 245, 273, 278, 281, 293, 307, 324, 333
    toward Christ 165, 256
    Christian 210, 216, 225, 240
    of God 139, 187, 210
love feast 170
Luther, Martin 253, 257, 258

marriage 159
martyrdom 220
Mass 195, 253, 258
meal, commemorative 165, 167
    common 166, 319
meditation 133, 324

memorial, Lord's Supper as 113, 121, 234, 305 [*see* Christ, remembering of]
memory 173
messianic banquet 119, 167, 168, 225, 229, 231-234
miracle 160, 162, 206
missions and missionary 170, 223-225, 236
multitude, feeding the 162, 313, 315
mystery, in religion 107

nature, sacramental character of 156

"Ordo Romanus Primus" 151

parable, Lord's Supper as 146
Paschal Lamb, Christ as 184, 274
Passover 127, 179, 211, 230
Passover cup 127
Pentecost 131, 200
persecution 220, 223
Peter 244
Pilate 244
Polycarp 220
prayer, fellowship of 200
priest, Christ as 138, 319
prison 228
prophet, Christ as 138
Protestantism, Lord's Supper in 148, 253-258

quarreling 247

Reformation 253, 257, 258
religion, joy in 251
    as luxury 150
    mystery in 107
    reality in 121
religious feelings 163
rest 294, 295

sacramental committal 196
sacramental community 207
sacramental life 159, 162, 164
sacramental universe 155
sacraments, antiquity of 157
    Christ's teaching of 155
    Christocentric view of 161
    church and 207
    food as 319
    Lord's Supper as 117
    meaning of 160
    misunderstanding of 123
    Protestant 159
    purpose of 163
    as signs of grace 207
    symbol and 164, 207
    Word and 157
sacrifice 319
    of Christ 154, 175, 178, 181-
        185, 258, 314
    of the church 186
saints, communion of 110, 210,
        321
self-examination 263-267
self-giving 147, 319
    of Christ 139, 142, 154, 243,
        282, 316
selfishness 264
self-sacrifice 147
sermon 160
servant, Christ as 236-239
sharing 326
sin, forgiveness of 111, 175, 183,
        225, 296, 302, 314
"social sacraments" 207
society, Christian 216
soul, attitude of 150
spirit, body and 148
Spirit, fellowship in the 201
spiritual adequacy 131
spiritual aspirations 170
spiritual awareness 155
spiritual nourishment 144
suffering 325

symbol, meaning of 152, 308
    power of 153, 155
    sacrament and 164, 207
symbolism, of Lord's Supper 104,
        108, 143, 144, 146, 149,
        154

table, of Christ 136, 139, 322
    fellowship of 167, 168, 171
thanksgiving, Lord's Supper as
        111, 112, 114, 117
"togetherness" 207
transubstantiation, doctrine of 120

unity, in Christ 206, 211, 216,
        228, 233, 256, 301, 311
    Christian 200, 209, 211, 212,
        216, 228, 256, 301, 311,
        321
    of the church 206, 207, 212,
        216, 228, 321
    sacrament of 321
universe, sacramental 155
unworthiness 295, 302, 306
Upper Room 106, 109, 122, 124,
        126-133, 139, 166, 211,
        215, 216, 231, 248, 270,
        310, 328

Vinci, Leonardo da 259-262
vine, discourse on the 117, 176,
        240, 325

washing, of disciples' feet 126,
        236-240, 279, 280
Washington, George 222
Wesley, John 253
wine 120, 143-151, 182, 189, 206
Word, sacraments and 157
    visible 110
World War I 226, 227
worship 212
    Lord's Supper and 108, 109,
        111

Zwingli, Ulrich 258